LITTLE BOOK OF BIG IDEAS

Business

First published in the United States of America in 2008
by Chicago Review Press, Incorporated
814 North Franklin Street
Chicago, Illinois 60610

Conceived and produced by
Elwin Street Limited
144 Liverpool Road
London N1 1LA
United Kingdom
www.elwinstreet.com

Illustrations: Richard Burgess and Emma Farrarons
Designer: Thomas Keenes

ISBN-13: 978-1-55652-749-4
ISBN-10: 1-55652-749-7

Printed in China

LITTLE BOOK OF BIG IDEAS

Business

John Lipczynski

CHICAGO
REVIEW
PRESS

Contents

Introduction

Very few people in the developed world are totally self-sufficient in the provision of their basic needs: food, clothing, and shelter. Instead, most of us depend on businesses to supply the goods and services essential to our everyday lives. Each day we make decisions as to what goods and services to buy, and this invariably involves us in transactions with many businesses. The coffee we drink for breakfast, the newspaper we read, the TV channel we watch, the train or car we take to work have all been produced by a business and have been selected by us from a wide variety of competing products.

Moreover, in the developed world, we do not just see our needs in terms of simple survival, but in terms of our standard of living. This standard is based on what we expect to be available to us, in relation to other groups in society. These expectations generate further demands on businesses that they are keen to supply, motivated by the eternal need to generate profit. Business is shaped by the demands of society—that is, by each one of us— and the most successful businesses shape our demands in turn.

There are certain key skills that those involved in business must possess in order to accomplish this. First, they must acquire the ownership of resources with which products and services can be produced. These resources are typically a workforce, capital equipment, premises, and raw materials. Second, they must ensure that these resources are financially secured before the sale of the output. This means that an entrepreneur must find capital with which to start the business—either from their own resources or by borrowing from other individuals or institutions. The third skill is to decide what to produce and in what quantities, and to coordinate the resources efficiently to achieve this production.

Business managers must constantly consider the competing alternatives for their resources—can their assets be used to create greater profits by producing something else? Finally and most importantly, businesses must anticipate future conditions of demand and supply in the marketplace. It is this last skill that distinguishes successful businessmen and women from those likely to fail. The most successful businesspeople are innovators, able to recognize and exploit the potential of untapped or growing markets.

The businesspeople chosen for this book are all considered to have influenced and changed the nature of global business. They have been responsible for an infusion of innovation that has left the business community better able to understand and exploit market conditions, and serve society more efficiently than before. Naturally any such selection of people is to some extent subjective and undoubtedly good arguments could be made for the inclusion of some other candidates. Nonetheless, the fifty people covered in this book are certainly in that elite group who have made an indelible mark on business theory and practice.

John Lipczynski

Ray Kroc

Ray Kroc realized in the 1950s that eating habits were undergoing a revolutionary change. More and more, people were eager to eat out rather than stay at home. However, people were often uncomfortable with the codes and etiquette of traditional restaurants. McDonald's provided a simple menu with a good service at low prices to reassure this new growing market. One went to McDonald's to eat, rather than to dine.

Born: 1902, Oak Park, Illinois
Importance: Created a new industry, fast food
Died: 1984, San Diego, California

As a 50-year-old salesman of milkshake machines, Kroc was intrigued to receive yet another order from a Californian hamburger outlet run by the McDonald brothers who had already bought eight such mixers. In 1954 Kroc traveled to California to see the McDonald operation. He saw clean premises staffed by white-clad servers speedily producing burgers at a low price. Seating was at a minimum and tableware nonexistent. He also noted the large lines snaking around the building. The McDonald brothers had introduced efficiency to an industry notorious for its casual manner and poor performance.

With his years of experience as a salesman, Kroc saw the potential for exporting the business around the country. Having agreed on a franchise arrangement with the brothers, he opened his Chicago branch of the restaurant in 1955, and the business was as successful in Illinois as in California. He opened two more franchises a year later, and by 1960 over 200 establishments were trading nationwide. In 1961 he bought out the brothers for $2.7 million thus leaving him free to develop the business unhindered.

Kroc knew that if the chain were to prosper, he would have to introduce greater standardization and greater efficiencies.

Standardization of the product, the service, and the ambience meant that these could be exported around the country and eventually around the world. He essentially mirrored Henry Ford's production process by linking precision to an efficient assembly line. All the products in the outlets were strictly specified so that each burger had a given weight and diameter and was accompanied by a given number of onions and pickles. By selling his franchisees an operating system, Kroc was able to brand his service. Customers realized that the experience of eating a McDonald's burger in Los Angeles could be replicated by a McDonald's burger in New York or indeed anywhere else. Kroc's stated aim was to "ensure repeat business is based on the system's reputation rather than on the quality of a single store or operator."

> "The two most important requirements for major success are: first, being in the right place at the right time, and second, doing something about it."
>
> Ray Kroc

The success of McDonald's was also possible due to the franchising of the outlets and its intense advertising. Kroc was very careful when choosing people to run the operation, typically choosing salesmen over accountants and chefs since they were good at developing a relationship with customers. The organization also invested heavily in both local and national advertising, which led to yet more growth. By the early 1970s, there were over 2,000 McDonald's branches in America with sales of over $1 billion. In the last three decades of the 20th century, the business moved into over 100 foreign markets.

Thomas Edison

Thomas Edison recognized the importance of inventions and innovations for the success of a business. He pursued his activities not necessarily in order to create something new, but because the results could be sold in the marketplace. In the space of some 60 years, he had accumulated over 1,000 patents and had made a dramatic impact on everyday life.

Born: 1847, Milan, Ohio
Importance: Developed a system of constant innovatory output
Died: 1931, New Jersey

Edison had little formal education, but, with sound home teaching and a natural curiosity, he was able to conduct basic science experiments as a child. As a 16-year-old telegraph operator, he focused his attention on examining the science of electrical machinery. In his early 20s he moved to Boston and then to New Jersey to become a full-time inventor. Over the next 30 years, Edison developed and patented an astonishing number of inventions. The most notable of these were the carbon telephone transmitter, the phonograph, the incandescent light bulb, the central power station, the alkaline storage battery, and motion pictures.

In 1879, Edison opened his first commercial laboratory in Menlo Park, New Jersey. In this "inventions factory," he applied economies of large-scale operations to the process of invention and innovation. This rewarded him with an efficient and constant flow of new technology. He became known as the "Wizard of Menlo Park." In 1887, Edison moved to larger premises in West Orange, where he developed improvements to existing products, such as a new phonograph, using a sound-impressed disk instead of a cylinder, and the development of the first talking movies in 1913.

Edison was truly entrepreneurial in his approach to business. Not only did he develop new products, but he was also

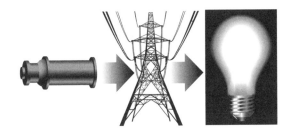

Above: Edison not only created items of great utility but also strengthened his own markets by manufacturing complementary products. To use a lightbulb required wiring, an electrical grid, and power stations—all of which Edison researched, manufactured, and sold.

responsible for their manufacture and distribution. He was quick to exploit this fact, realizing, for example, that central electric power plants were important to the sales of light bulbs. These plants required components that were developed and manufactured by Edison's industries. In 1882, he built the first electric power station in Manhattan's financial district.

Edison was considered a ruthless businessman, often getting involved in patent litigation and petty squabbles with competitors. One such example is the case of electric power generation, where he backed direct current (DC) power as opposed to the more efficient alternating current (AC) power championed by archrival George Westinghouse. Edison believed AC to be more dangerous and went as far as publicly electrocuting an elephant to prove his point.

Above all, Thomas Edison was more innovator than inventor. He looked at existing ideas and tried to improve them with the hope of exploiting them commercially. The ticker tape machine, the telephone, the telegraph, and the light bulb had all been improved by Edison for practical use. In this sense he was a businessman first and a scientist second.

John Jacob Astor

John Jacob Astor was one of the first truly diversified capitalists in the United States. He enjoyed great success in the fur business, for which he is best known, and was able to identify and exploit the concept of international trade well before any potential rival, amassing vast wealth. He was also successful in finance and real estate.

Born: 1763, Waldorf, Germany
Importance: Demonstrated a shrewd knowledge of international trade
Died: 1848, New York

Astor was born in Germany and as a young man was sent by his family to London to help his brother, a trader in musical instruments. He emigrated to America in 1784 and found employment with a furrier in New York. Within a few years he was back in London selling furs, while shipping musical instruments back to New York, becoming America's first established retailer of such goods. By the end of the 18th century, apart from his fur business interests, Astor had investments in banks, an insurance company, and real estate. His trade also expanded to include arms, wool, and opium.

It was the fur business, however, that attracted Astor the most. In 1808, he founded the American Fur Company and established trading posts along the Missouri and Columbia rivers. He decided to compete with established monopolies, such as the British Hudson Bay Company in Canada, and succeeded in doing so by building good relations with the native Indians and the British, who gave him permission to trade. His success was partly due to his ability to exert considerable political control over key American and British politicians. For example, during the War of 1812, Astor's fur trade was disrupted following the British capture of many of his trading posts. Within five years, however, with the help of protectionist measures from the U.S. Congress, he managed to reestablish the near monopoly status of his company around the Great Lakes.

Astor's skill was in identifying comparative advantage between regions and countries. A comparative advantage exists for two parties when one has a lower relative cost of producing a product or service than the other and can specialize in its production. Such specialization is only possible if trade is taking place. Astor, as an entrepreneur controlling many different businesses, was in a position to exploit such advantages. His enterprise was vast. Through his trading posts, Astor bought furs directly from the Indians in exchange for household items and alcohol. The furs were exported to Europe and China in ships owned by Astor and traded for luxury European and Chinese goods, which Astor then imported and sold in New York.

Astor became so wealthy that he even managed to underwrite government borrowing needed to finance the War of 1812. In 1816, he was also involved in the creation of the Second Bank of the United States, further extending his power in the political arena. By the mid 1830s, Astor retired from the fur business and began to invest his profits in real estate ventures around the Manhattan area. He also

> "If I could live all over again, I would buy every square inch of Manhattan."
>
> Astor from his deathbed

funded various philanthropic works. On his deathbed Astor claimed that, were he to relive his life, he would invest every dollar he had into buying property on Manhattan Island. By the time of his death, it was reported that his fortune stood at $20 million, making him the richest man in the United States.

Frederick Winslow Taylor

Having failed to get into Harvard due to severe eyestrain, Taylor went to work at the Midvale Steel Works, where he became a foreman, chief draftsman, research director, and chief engineer. His goal in each post was to work out how production tasks could be completed more efficiently.

Born: 1856, Philadelphia, Pennsylvania
Importance: Developed working methods that extracted greater measurable efficiency from the workforce
Died: 1915, Philadelphia, Pennsylvania

With his firsthand experience of poor working practices and "rule of thumb" management in large industry, Taylor attempted to redress losses in efficiency by implementing "scientific management." At the core of this new approach was task allocation—breaking down the overall production process into smaller component parts, subjecting each to time-and-motion studies, and assigning them to specific workers with set targets. Incentives were provided by a system of rewards and penalties— hence the slogan "pay the person not the job." Taylor also argued that training the workforce to achieve specific targets was an extremely important motivating factor.

One barrier to the successful implementation of scientific management was the poor level of English and general education of newly arrived immigrant workers. Taylor determined that foremen and workers with limited education should not be in a position to decide how a particular job was best carried out. He solved the problem by separating the planning from the execution. To achieve this, he created planning departments, whose task was to measure and analyze the work and then set realistic targets. He was able to double productivity at Midvale.

As his reputation and success spread, Taylor soon found consulting work in other manufacturing enterprises. In 1901, he

Above: One of Taylor's time studies involved the size of a shovel. By careful experimentation, he determined the weight of the most efficient shovel-load—any more and the load takes too long to shovel; any less and too many shoveling actions are required. He even went as far as developing shovels that would carry this exact amount.

carried out a major cost analysis of production methods at Bethlehem Steel that reduced the productive workforce from 500 men to just 140, lowered the cost of materials handled from eight cents to four, *and* doubled production. However, his radical methods brought opposition from middle management and trade unions. The foremen and managers felt marginalized by the bevy of researchers and analysts on the shop floor, while organized labor feared for their jobs. Taylor lost his position at Bethlehem and was never to work in industry again.

Scientific management has been a source of much debate over the past 100 years. There are those who have criticized Taylorism for its patronizing attitude toward the workforce, which allows no other contribution from the individual worker than his or her effort, and which ultimately leads to a de-motivated workforce. Modern management theorists stress the importance of individual worker input and teamwork. Others claim, however, that Taylor's views have been misinterpreted and that he placed the individual worker's interest as high as that of management.

Frank Woolworth

Despite his farm upbringing, Frank Woolworth always had aspirations to work in business. In 1873, he found employment with a dry goods store in Watertown, New York. When there was a downturn in trade, the shop decided to launch a promotion in which all the goods on a given shelf were priced at just five cents. Woolworth was given the task of selecting the goods and organizing their display. It proved to be a great success.

Born: 1852, New York
Importance: Introduced the five-and-dime discount stores
Died: 1919, New York

In 1878, with a loan and some advanced stock, Woolworth opened his own store in the back streets of Utica, New York, hoping to emulate his previous success at Watertown. All stock was priced at five cents—the first product was a five cent shovel. After some initial success, sales soon leveled off. Although the store had made enough for him to repay the start-up loans, Woolworth decided that, to have long-term success, his store needed to be in the heart of town to attract greater numbers of shoppers. In 1879, he opened a centrally located store in Lancaster, Pennsylvania, and expanded the range of goods to include a number priced at ten cents. The five-and-ten was born.

The enterprise proved a triumph, offering quality products—personally selected by Woolworth—attractive window and counter displays, and a surprisingly large range of goods at very affordable prices. Shoppers were allowed to browse the counters and to inspect the goods in their own time before making a purchase. In comparison to the traditional general store, where shoppers asked a clerk for products that were kept behind a counter, this was a retailing revolution. The stores were especially popular with new immigrants with low incomes and usually poor

English language skills, who were often intimidated by the traditional mode of shopping.

Woolworth decided to expand his business by opening other, similar, shops. He invited partner managers to invest half the money needed to fit out a new shop in return for half the profits when the shop opened. The number of investors grew in line with the success of the stores. Woolworth also developed partnerships with rival stores in order to create greater buying power and therefore maximize on volume discounts from the wholesalers. With certain goods, such as candy, he bypassed the wholesalers altogether, dealing directly with the manufacturers. These rival stores—Woolworth's so-called friendly rivals—also benefited from Woolworth's skills as a buyer, particularly when dealing with European suppliers, and he was renowned for his skills in striking a good deal. By 1912, having merged with his friendly rivals, Woolworth floated his new company, the F. W. Woolworth Company, raising $65 million. By the time of his death, in 1919, there were 1,000 stores across the country sporting the familiar red Woolworth logo.

With the outbreak of war in 1914, supplies from Europe were severely restricted. Woolworth decided to develop potentially cheaper domestic sources, based on the mass-manufacturing processes he had observed in Europe. He became an important contributor to the introduction of mass production in the United States for a wide variety of goods.

Supply chain: The sequence of processes by which a commodity is produced and distributed to consumers. In theory, the shorter the chain—i.e., the fewer links between raw materials and end user—the more profitable the process is. In practice, extra links in the chain, such as wholesalers, can create savings by applying economies of scale to transport and storage.

Innovation

Innovation can be defined as the introduction of superior qualities to products or methods of production that render existing products or processes obsolete. Innovation confers significant advantages on a firm, affecting output, product quality, employment, wages, and profit. It is also a major driving force behind economic growth and improvements in social welfare.

Innovation plays a key role in research and development, and can be subdivided into several different stages. The first is basic research, which might be considered as "inventive" activity. The second is applied research and development work, which might be strictly thought of as "innovative" activity. The last stage is the diffusion or spread of the new idea through the firm, the industry, and the economy.

The decision to invest in innovation is strategic, and is not determined exclusively by considerations of short-run profit maximization. There are a number of strategic issues that influence this type of investment.

An *offensive* strategy seeks to enable a firm to dominate its market through the introduction of a new technology. The main focus of activity within the firm is to generate new ideas and to protect these, and associated spin-offs, by acquiring patents. The firm invests heavily in capital equipment as well as developing the skills of its workforce. Major 20th-century innovations that were developed in this manner include DuPont's development of nylon (1928) and Lycra (1959), IG Farben's development of PVC (1929), and RCA's development of color television (1954). The firm may be willing to invest in basic research, although not of the purest type. In order to stay ahead of actual or potential competitors, the firm must undertake some experimental development work, and it requires a capability to design, build, and test prototypes and pilot plants.

A *defensive* strategy is one forced on firms in order to keep pace with product improvements or technical change initiated by competitors. If it does nothing, the firm's market share could collapse because rivals are able to offer more advanced products or sell at lower prices because their production costs are lower. The defensive firm may lack the large technical resources needed to pursue an offensive strategy, or it may be risk averse, preferring to invest only in proven products or processes. A defensive strategy may include efforts to introduce small improvements to existing technologies, permissible within the constraints of the patent breadth.

An *imitative* strategy allows a firm to copy ideas, either by acquiring a license in the short run or by exploiting free knowledge in the long run. For an imitative strategy to be profitable, the imitator must have some advantage that can be exploited, such as cheap labor or a captive market. For example, as well as increased competition from alternative products such as Orlon, Dacron, and nylon, a major reason for DuPont's withdrawal from the U.S. rayon market in 1960 was its inability to compete with the low-cost producers.

Finally, *dependent* strategies exist where firms accept subservient roles in relation to stronger offensive firms, perhaps as suppliers or subcontractors. They adopt technologies that are passed down to them, often accompanied by technical assistance and the loaning of skilled labor. This type of relationship is common in the Japanese electronics and car industries.

John MacArthur

Today, Australia is the largest sheep-producing country in the world, accounting for a quarter of the world's total supply with a value of around A$2.5 billion each year. Australian merino wool is regarded as the finest available. This record owes much to the efforts of John and Elizabeth MacArthur.

Born: 1766, Plymouth, England
Importance: Brought Australian wool to the world market
Died: 1834, Camden Park, New South Wales, Australia

John MacArthur joined the British Army at age 15 and, after his marriage to Elizabeth, was posted in 1789 to the New South Wales Corps in Sydney. In due course he was appointed paymaster for the new colony and, later, Inspector of Public Works. In 1793, he was given 100 acres (40 hectares) of land, an area subsequently increased, in recognition of the work he had undertaken in developing it (albeit with convict labor). A few years later MacArthur bought some merino sheep from South Africa.

The merino sheep had already been imported to Australia for its wool and meat and had a reputation for the quality of its thick, fine fleece. However, as a result of crossbreeding with the indigenous sheep, the quality of the Australian wool was considered poor. The MacArthurs decided not to crossbreed their stock and, by 1803, had amassed a flock of 4,000 near-pure merinos. To strengthen and improve the bloodline, they imported additional pure merinos. Much of this work was carried out by Elizabeth MacArthur, as her husband was frequently at odds with government officials. He was twice forced to return to England: first to face a court martial over a duel and, second, following his involvement in a rebellion. MacArthur put these absences to good use, however, buying up vast areas of land in New South Wales and traveling throughout Europe to sell his wool.

MacArthur realized that the enormous potential of the Australian wool industry was held back by its reputation for a low quality product. By dramatically improving the quality, and aggressively promoting the improvement in his target markets, MacArthur arguably created one of the first international brands.

Wool was a perfect export for Australia (ideal products for shipping to Europe needed to be both nonperishable and maintain a high value by weight) and provided a great boost to its economy. Furthermore, the Napoleonic Wars of the early 19th century saw a reduction in the supply of wool from Spain, Britain's traditional source. In consequence the demand for quality Australian wool soared, and with it the price. Exports to Britain made the MacArthurs extremely rich.

On his return to Australia in 1817, MacArthur continued to develop his farming, diversified into commercial wine production, and became involved in the Bank of Australia. Another of his pet projects was the establishment of a chartered company to organize the production of wool. The Australian Agricultural Company was set up in London in 1824 with a capital of £1 million and a million acres of land and the objective of raising fine wool sheep in New South Wales. Within a year it was also involved in coal mining, making use of harbor facilities at the nearby port of Newcastle. The company exists to this day.

Chartered company:
A business formed under a government charter or license, granting specific rights to exploit a given territory or resource, often under certain conditions. Such companies were often formed by colonial governments to allow development of a new territory or resource, without losing control of the manner in which it was exploited.

Charles Babbage

Babbage is considered the father of computers because of his research into computing machines. Although none of his machines were ever fully operational, owing to a lack of funding, Babbage's manufacturing experience led him to develop theories of production efficiency that have influenced generations of economists and business analysts.

Born: 1791, Teignmouth, Devonshire, England
Importance: Responsible for the development of programmable calculating machines, and an early theorist of production economics
Died: 1871, London, England

Babbage had always been bothered by the high level of error in calculation by mathematical tables, such as logarithms, so after becoming Lucasian Professor of Mathematics at Cambridge University, he sought to develop a machine that could take the drudgery out of the calculations and remove human error.

In 1820, he developed a prototype "difference engine," a mechanical calculating device. The initial promise of the investment attracted government funding, but, over time, as problems with design and construction mounted, this funding was gradually withdrawn. Undaunted, Babbage moved on to a more ambitious project, the analytical engine, precursor to the programmable computer. Once again, the practicalities of manufacturing such a machine defeated the capabilities of Victorian engineering.

Frustrated by the unavailability of precision engineering required for his two computing machines, Babbage built a forge in his house and, together with his draftsmen, designed new lathes and introduced a standard system of screw threads, both of which advanced the British machine-tools industry considerably. He also wrote a guide to life insurance, developed a system of lighthouse signaling, devised a method of code breaking, introduced standard railroad gauges, and even forms, and employed salesmen to play up his customers' perception of high-quality pottery as a symbol of social status. Above all else, he developed the name of Wedgwood as a brand and ensured that it was printed on every item of his pottery and china, to guarantee its source and thus its quality.

It was crucial to this strategy that the products be of the highest standard, to preserve the reputation of the brand. Stories abound of his visiting workshops and smashing vessels of poor quality with his stick, shouting "this will not do for Josiah Wedgwood"—an early example of quality control to protect the brand image. This branding gave the product more value than its simple utility—a Wedgwood dinner set was a sign of social status, extremely important to the newly affluent middle class.

> "Fashion is infinitely superior to merit in many respects."
>
> letter to Thomas Bentley, 1779

In the early 1770s, a depression hit the economy. Demand for high-quality goods fell, stock levels rose, and prices had to be cut. Wedgwood faced a financial crisis. He responded by revolutionizing the way his business was costed. He ensured that up-to-date accounts were kept of labor and material costs, and that a proper calculation was made of all overheads. He found that certain products were more costly to produce than others, and, where possible, increased their prices to compensate. Potential economies of scale were measured, and unit costs were reduced by expanding the volume of output. Most importantly, he priced his output in response to demand. As a result of these reforms, Wedgwood's business survived the depression, while many of his rivals did not.

Richard Arkwright

Blessed with an ability to identify the potential of other people's ideas, Richard Arkwright was primarily an innovator rather than an inventor. He developed machinery that not only accelerated the production of yarn and thread for the textile industry but also resulted in yarn of better quality. Moreover, by locating large-scale industrial activity under one roof, he predicted the modern factory system.

Born: 1732, Preston, England
Importance: Developed the factory system of manufacture
Died: 1792, Nottingham, England

Arkwright started his business career in wig making. When the fashion for wigs waned, he turned his attention to textiles—in particular to the problem of spinning yarn efficiently. Spinning was traditionally carried out in private houses using a foot-operated wheel. The process was slow and could not keep up with the pace of knitters and weavers. For large-scale production, James Hargreaves had already developed the spinning jenny in 1764, but this machine required skilled labor and was unreliable.

In 1768, Arkwright met a clockmaker, John Kay, and together they produced a spinning machine, or frame, initially powered by horses. Further modifications replaced the horsepower with waterpower and the machines became better known as water frames. The advantage of this machine was not simply that it produced a stronger, finer thread, but that it could be operated by cheap, unskilled labor (primarily children and young adults).

The first water-powered mill was established in 1771 at Cromford in Derbyshire, England. Given the scale of the industrial production, the mill had to employ hundreds of workers. At its peak, 1,900 people worked at Cromford. The factory system had arrived. To attract these workers, Arkwright built cottages around the mill and a community soon developed. Further refinements in

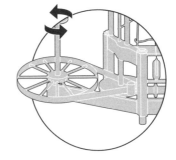

Above: Arkwright replaced manpower—used to turn the spindles of his competitor's spinning jenny—with horsepower and, later, waterpower. This allowed his machines to be operated by children, who drew lower wages than adult workers.

the manufacturing process were added, chiefly in post-spinning activities such as carding and cleaning. Another innovation was the application of steam power to pump the water. The mill proved a great financial success and, in time, the textiles produced by this method became one of Britain's main exports.

With his innovations protected by patents, Arkwright was able to build other, equally successful, mills around the country. Some of these patents were later revoked when it was shown, in court, that he had copied the ideas of other innovators, but by then the process was well established. Arkwright was knighted in 1786 and, on his death, his personal fortune was estimated at £500,000—a substantial sum for that time.

With the application of new technology, and by linking it with different processes on a massive scale in one plant, Arkwright was responsible for the development of the modern factory system. This became a characteristic feature of the Industrial Revolution, copied in many other industries and eventually around the world.

William Cockerill

William Cockerill began his career as an engineer, building machines used in the wool industry—spinning jennies, flying shuttles, and looms. In 1799, he emigrated to the town of Verviers, Belgium, where he established himself primarily as a producer of textile machinery. By importing British technology and know-how, he kick-started the Industrial Revolution in Belgium and France.

Born: 1759, Lancashire, England
Importance: Introduced British textile technology to Europe
Died: 1832, Aachen, Germany

Cockerill's European career began in 1794 in St. Petersburg, Russia, where he worked for Catherine II. Failure to fulfill a contract led to his imprisonment, but he managed to escape and arrived in Belgium in 1799 with his three sons. He settled in the town of Verviers, an established center of the Belgian textile industry, where he built workshops for the construction of spinning and wool-carding machines vertically integrated (see page 37) with iron-making facilities to provide the raw material for their manufacture. So great was his success that he exported machines all over Europe and was able to establish a textile factory in Liège in 1807.

In 1817, having passed the day-to-day running of the business to his son John, William oversaw the development and equipping of the largest iron foundry in Europe, located at Seraing, southwest of Liège. The production of large quantities of cast iron allowed the

"Cockerill settled in Belgium and supplied excellent machinery, which allowed [it] to achieve a precocious, fast, and perfect Industrial Revolution, without much trial and error."

F. Crouxet

Cockerills to tap into new export markets, chiefly in the railroad, armament, and bridge-building industries. By expanding their focus to export markets across Europe, they were able to produce and sell on a much larger scale than would have been possible had they confined themselves to the demands of the local Belgian market. As a result they produced and ran machinery on a much larger scale. The average horsepower (hp) of a machine produced at Seraing was 145, while rivals, producing mostly for the local market, produced much smaller machines, averaging just 20 hp. This advantage allowed the Seraing plant to enjoy lower average costs of production—in other words, higher economies of large-scale production.

The significance of Cockerill's impact on the economies of France and the Low Countries was that by manufacturing textile machines "in situ," he managed to import a technology without physically having to import British machines. (Britain had, at that time, strict controls on the export of textile machinery to Europe to protect her competitive advantage.) The Cockerill strategy of establishing an enterprise and exporting from the Continent led to a diffusion of British manufacturing technology and know-how—a strategy that was copied by entrepreneurs in other industries.

As a result, Belgium and northern France were able to enjoy a very quick, and almost seamless, Industrial Revolution without all the associated economic and social upheavals experienced in Britain. Not only did their economies profit from cheaper costs of production—owing mostly to the low average wage of the new urban proletariat—but they also enjoyed the benefits of tried-and-true technology, which directly integrated into the developing manufacturing economy.

The Production Line

A production line is the method by which input is transformed into output following a sequential operation of tasks. Each task adds value by further refining the article until it reaches the stage at which it can be marketed. The efficiency of the operation is determined by the available technology and the extent of central coordination.

At its most basic, a production line is a simple sequence of events that transforms raw materials into finished goods. In most cases, it is possible for one worker to perform all the necessary discrete tasks. However, with better organization, savings in production are made by arranging labor into groups, each of which specializes in the completion of just one aspect of the overall process.

History has many examples of this process of manufacturing, including chariot construction in ancient Egypt, crossbow production in ancient China, and boat building in 16th-century Venice. Most of these resulted from a government demand to equip its armed forces. In contrast, what we recognize as a production line today came about in a bid to meet the mass consumption of the growing urban proletariat of the 19th century. It was made possible by the development of steam power, new machinery, an efficient transportation network, and the introduction of the factory system. The key to the modern method of production was that a product could be broken down into its integrated parts, which were then copied precisely using accurate technical drawings. This allowed workers to produce a part they had not made or seen before.

The revolution of working this way was that it no longer depended on individual strength or technical skill. This meant that nontraditional groups in society (mostly women and children) could now work in factories and make a positive contribution to productivity. With the technical advances of the machine-tools industry, it was possible to produce standardized and interchangeable components, each part being identical to all other parts. This transformed the production line into an "assembly line," which eventually became the "automated" assembly line, as introduced by Henry Ford in Detroit (see pages 34–35).

The economics of the continuous-flow assembly line were based on bringing the work to the worker, thus making as full use of the worker's time as possible. In a craft industry, for example, the worker spends a lot of time looking for parts and tools and walking from one machine to the next. On the assembly line, however, one worker repeats a near-identical operation, on an exact replica of a part, using the same conveniently located tool. Furthermore, as most of the task is carried out by machines, there is less scope for human error and variability of the output.

A drawback of the system is that production—which is geared to standardization—is inflexible when faced with a market that requires greater product differentiation. Goods based on fashion and style are not attractive for this system of production, for example. A further drawback is an alienated and demoralized workforce that may dislike the homogenization of work and the inherent de-skilling. In the last three decades, industry has moved away from the traditional assembly-line method of production, and toward newer approaches of "total quality management," "just-in-time" stock controls, and "leaderless work groups."

Alfred Krupp

Alfred Krupp followed his father into the family steelmaking business, which he expanded in an unprecedented way. He invested in new technology, most notably the new "Bessemer process," and vertically integrated into coal mining in Germany and France. He also diversified his output into the production of railroad stock and armaments for foreign governments.

Born: 1812, Essen, Germany
Importance: Recognized the full potential of cast steel
Died: 1887, Essen, Germany

Alfred Krupp's father died when Alfred was 14, forcing him to abandon his schooling in order to help run his father's small steel foundary in Essen, Germany, producing cast steel, tools, and coin dyes. For the next 15 years the business struggled on, with Krupp working alongside his workers in the plant. By night he carried on his father's research into perfecting the casting of solid-steel blocks. In 1848, he became the sole owner of the business, which at the time employed just over 100 people.

The years he spent trying to improve the steel products began to bear fruit. In 1847, he built a muzzle-loading gun of cast steel, as opposed to the traditional bronze, and, in 1851, he exhibited a two-ton, flawless, cast-steel ingot at London's Great Exhibition. As a result, Krupp's Essen plant became famous throughout the world.

The business specialized in the production of good-quality cast steel for railroad stock—notably weldless wheel tires. By the late 1850s, the business had branched into the manufacture of steel cannons, and these soon began to dominate output—partly owing to the decline in demand for nonmilitary products and partly thanks to generous government subsidies for munitions, in the nervous political environment of Europe in the late 19th century. By the time of Krupp's death, the production of military goods, mostly artillery, accounted for about 50 percent of the total output of Krupp's enterprises, thereby giving rise to his nickname "the Cannon King."

To ensure that his plants had a steady, and assured, supply of raw materials, Krupp vertically integrated his steel production into the coal and iron industries. At the same time, he made sure that the business was up to date technologically, manufacturing steel products cost-effectively and of the highest quality. He was also very successful in looking after his workforce. He built special "colonies" for his workers, provided educational and social facilities, and even set up a system of welfare benefits and pensions. Although today this approach might appear highly paternalistic (for example, he forbade workers to get involved in politics), he managed to generate a high degree of loyalty from his employees. By the 1880s the company employed 20,000 workers.

One further success can be ascribed to Krupp. He ensured that the business would survive his death by establishing two principles: first, that earnings should be reinvested into the business and, second, that the company was to be run by a single heir.

"We have, from the first, been loyal to one another and care for welfare, justice, and strict impartiality towards all creeds have been repaid by zealous work and devotion…That is the explanation of the prosperity of the whole Works."

Alfred Krupp

Henry Ford

Henry Ford transformed 19th-century manufacturing into the efficient mass-production we see today. He not only revolutionized production processes but also changed American society: the mass-market automobile enabled increased mobility, leading to the growth of cities, suburban centers, and a network of highways.

Born: 1863, Detroit, Michigan
Importance: Introduced the moving assembly line to large-scale manufacturing
Died: 1947, Dearborn, Michigan

Ford came into the automobile industry through a long apprenticeship in mechanical engineering, which ended with his ownership of a company that built racing cars. The relative success of Ford's designs attracted investors and, in 1903, the Ford Motor Company was incorporated (see pages 42–43). Immediately there were tensions in the new company, as the majority of the investors were interested in the production of high-quality and expensive automobiles, while Ford argued for producing cheap automobiles in high numbers. By 1908, having successfully bought out the fellow shareholders, Ford produced the Model T for an affordable $850. In time, the price fell as low as $280, with Ford selling more than 15 million automobiles in the United States over the next 20 years.

The low prices were the result of great reductions in the unit costs of production. The dominant production process prior to the Ford Motor Company's innovations was for one team of workers to build an automobile in situ from top to bottom. At Ford, the production of the automobile was divided into a number of discrete tasks—84 in the case of the Model T—and each worker focused his efforts on just one task. In addition, Ford improved the flow of production. As one task was completed, the next followed immediately, with no loss of time in between.

Above: In Ford's production line, each worker remains at a station and the cars move from station to station along the line. By dividing the manufacturing process into discrete parts and having each worker manage only one of these tasks, Ford was able to employ less skilled labor and increase productivity.

Cars were placed on a conveyor belt and production moved seamlessly in time with the completion of each task: the moving assembly line had arrived. By 1914, Ford's plant could produce an automobile in 93 minutes—eight times faster than older methods—and a new vehicle rolled out of the plant every 24 seconds.

Vertical integration ensured further efficiency through the purchase of businesses such as railroads, coal and iron ore mines, saw mills, glassworks, rubber plantations, and the development of dealer franchises.

A major problem for early mass producers was low morale among the labor force. Labor turnover prior to 1914 averaged around 50 percent of the workforce. However, Ford doubled the hourly wage from the industry rate of $2.50 to $5.00, to ensure his workforce was settled and motivated. Ford realized that his workers were also his potential customers: paying them a good wage helped to stimulate demand for the product of their labor. This strategy became known as Fordism.

Andrew Carnegie

Carnegie's career began in the iron industry. Attracted by the potential of the Bessemer process (the first economical method of converting pig iron into steel), he decided to invest in a steel plant near Pittsburgh. Carnegie realized that the future of heavy industry lay in the use of steel. The success of the plant made Carnegie one of America's richest men.

Born: 1835, Dunfermline, Scotland
Importance: Greatly expanded the American steel industry
Died: 1919, Lenox, Massachusetts

Seeking to escape poverty in Scotland, the Carnegie family emigrated to Pittsburgh in 1848. By 1853, the young Andrew found employment with the Pennsylvania Railroad and was involved in military transportation during the Civil War (1861–1865). Seeing the demand for iron created by the war, Carnegie resigned from the railroad company and invested in a business replacing wooden bridges with iron ones. Within three years he was earning $50,000 a year. Carnegie also acquired blast furnaces, iron mills, oil fields, and locomotive works and acted as broker of railroad bonds.

On one of his regular trips to Britain, he met Henry Bessemer, the inventor of the much-admired steel converter. Carnegie was convinced that the future of industry—in construction, railroads, shipbuilding, and armaments—lay in steel. In 1874, he and his partners built a Bessemer plant in Pittsburgh. Always quick to adopt cost-saving innovations, by the 1890s, Carnegie had adopted the more efficient open-hearth furnace method. He also explored the potential efficiency of vertical integration, buying coke fields and iron-ore mines to provide raw materials, and ships and railroads to transport both the materials and the finished products. In 1889, the assets of the enterprise were consolidated into the Carnegie Steel Company.

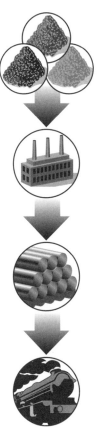

The company was a financial success and expanded greatly. Production of steel between 1889 and 1899 rose from 300,000 tons to 2.6 million tons. However, there was a potential conflict with his partner Henry Frick, who was by this time in managerial control of the company. In 1899, Carnegie bought him out for $15 million. By 1901, Frick had teamed up with the banker J. P. Morgan (see pages 62–63), and they bought the company for $500 million, making Carnegie a fortune of $225 million. The company was renamed U.S. Steel Corporation and was capitalized at around $1.4 billion, one of the largest companies in the world.

After 1901, Carnegie turned to disposing of his fortune with the same vigor he had shown in amassing it. He spent his money on public libraries, universities, hospitals, and in funding scientific research. It was estimated that he had given away some $350 million by the time of his death.

Cornelius Vanderbilt

From a modest start, operating a ferry business in New York Harbor with just one boat, Cornelius Vanderbilt progressed to steamships and offered a successful transport service along the Hudson River and East Coast that was both competitive and renowned for its quality. In the second phase of his business career, he acquired various railroad companies and went on to dominate the market in northeast America.

Born: 1794, New York
Importance: Pioneered low-cost, high-quality transport
Died: 1877, New York

At just 16, Vanderbilt was already operating a ferry service between Staten Island and Manhattan in New York. In the War of 1812, he profited from a government contract to provide fortifications around New York. He used these profits to expand his shipping interests, establishing himself as the owner of a steamboat working for a ferry service along the Hudson River. With a strategy he was to follow in later years, he undercut the competition, charging $1 to their $4 and offering better and more comfortable service. Vanderbilt's boss was sued by outraged rivals who had been granted a legal monopoly, but the court ruled against the plaintiffs and left Vanderbilt free to dominate traffic along the Hudson. By 1829, he was working independently and, again, found great success, usually by severely undercutting his rivals. By the 1840s he had over 100 boats and a personal fortune estimated at $500,000.

In 1849, he offered a cheaper and quicker ferry route across Central America for people wishing to join in the California Gold Rush. Soon after, although with less success, he built three ships to challenge the Cunard (see pages 40–41) and Collins Lines across the North Atlantic. Once again his tactic was to attract volume by cutting prices. In this instance the service just about broke even, and by 1861 Vanderbilt had sold the business.

Railroad companies now became Vanderbilt's focus. He started with the New York and Harlem Railroad, which, through a series of acquisitions and consolidations, became extremely profitable. This success stemmed partly from the sheer volume of customers, but also from Vanderbilt's continual investment in the infrastructure—introducing steel rails for the most frequently used routes, for example, and quadruple tracks, which allowed passenger and freight traffic to run separately.

Vanderbilt was hard working and extremely careful with his money. He was not known for great philanthropy and, on his death, he willed the bulk of his fortune to one son, William, leaving two other sons with no inheritance at all.

In business he could master details very quickly and determine appropriate, successful strategies. In particular, he triumphed at charging low prices for a quality service. This was possible for two reasons. First, the prices charged by dominant producers were often kept artificially high, protected by state monopolies and quasi-cartel agreements. Second, where no such monopolies were enjoyed, Vanderbilt's pricing was ruthlessly designed to destroy the competition, even at the cost of a short-term loss. By offering a cheaper service with no reduction in quality, he was able to undermine competitors, and to ensure loyalty from his customers in the face of future competition.

> "I have been insane on the subject of moneymaking all my life."
>
> Cornelius Vanderbilt

Samuel Cunard

The son of a timber merchant, Samuel Cunard joined the family business and saw it expand into banking, lumber, shipbuilding, and shipping. With an interest in steam navigation, he won the government tender to carry mail across the North Atlantic. In 1840, with four ships, he established a regular service between England and North America that soon earned a reputation for its speed and safety.

Born: 1787, Halifax, Nova Scotia, Canada
Importance: Founder of the Cunard Line, the most famous ocean line in history
Died: 1865, London, England

Lacking a formal education, and thus the chance of joining one of the professions, Cunard turned to an obvious career—trade. An early background in his father's timber business had already taught him some basic knowledge of commerce and finance and how to make a profit. For an ambitious young businessman, the opportunities in Halifax, Nova Scotia, were dominated by seaborne commerce, and it is little surprise that Cunard was drawn to this industry. His fortune was to win, against all odds, the colonial government contract to ferry mail from Halifax to Boston and the West Indies.

The admiralty had long regarded sail as an inefficient means of transporting mail and had stipulated that they would only consider steamships for the task. Everyone in the business assumed that the British Western Steamship Company would win the contract, as it already enjoyed a monopoly of steamship travel across the North Atlantic. Certain that no other rival was in a position to bid, the company asked for a delay in starting its service, in order to build more powerful ships than those stipulated in the tender. In the meantime, Cunard, among the first businessmen in Canada to invest in steamships, heard of the admiralty's tender. The attraction of operating on the world stage

Above: Cunard's initial fleet of four paddle steamers included the *SS Royal William*, the first ship to cross the Atlantic entirely under steam power. The crossing took around 14 days—not significantly faster than a sailing ship with a good wind, but more predictable in the face of uncertain weather.

was irresistible to Cunard. Reacting quickly and decisively, he managed to negotiate sufficient financial backing and to secure the assistance of Robert Napier, the foremost steamship engineer of his day, to tender for the job. The reliability of the service he offered impressed the authorities enough for him to win the contract.

Although Cunard faced some potentially strong competition—there was no shortage of firms wanting a share of the prestigious North Atlantic market—the company managed to survive. This was due mostly to the company's firm financial base as well as the advantages accruing to an incumbent firm and subsidies from the British Government. In due course the Cunard Line took over such companies as the Canadian Northern Steamship Company and the White Star Line, albeit after Samuel Cunard's death. His activities and achievements in a sense mirrored the early development and history of Atlantic Canada. The success of the business had complemented the relative economic success of the region.

The Incorporated Company

The act of "incorporation" creates a company with a separate legal identity. Thus, in the eyes of the law, the company is seen and treated as being distinct from its owners. The advantage is that the company's debts are not the owners' debts; owners' liability is limited only to their investments.

The most common business modules today are "sole ownership" and "partnership." Both are relatively easy to set up and tend to exist in businesses that require little start-up capital. There are, however, two disadvantages: expansion of the business is constrained by the finances the owners can raise, and they face unlimited liability should the business run into debt. Owners' personal assets are, therefore, always at risk.

The principal reason for incorporation is for the business to enjoy the advantages of a separate legal identity. This means that the company is able to own property, enter into contracts, sue and be sued, trade under its own name, and be taxed as a separate entity. Once incorporated, the company exists until it is wound up—either voluntarily or involuntarily—and therefore has a life that is independent of its owners.

An important consequence of the legal position is the limited liability enjoyed by the owners. Typically, in a public company, the owners are the shareholders. Their liability is limited to their shareholding. If the company goes bankrupt, shareholders' debts will only be limited to the unpaid amount of their shares, or if the shares are fully paid up on issue, they have no further liability. Historically this has proved a major attraction for potential investors. In reality, owners of little-known public companies, who may be involved in the managing of the business, are sometimes asked for personal guarantees by banks, which can then extend their liability to personal assets.

Incorporation also allows for the continuity of ownership and the transferability of interest. As the company's existence is separate from that of its owners, it survives their death or bankruptcy. Furthermore, since there is a ready market for shares, the owners have the ability to sell their interests, thus transferring them to different owners.

In the larger organization, incorporation usually results in the separation of ownership from control. The owners elect a board of directors who are charged with the responsibility of running the company. The duties of these officials—holding annual general meetings (AGMs) and presenting company accounts—are usually defined in statute.

There are some further advantages of incorporation that businesses may consider. First, a company has the right to a unique name and can therefore exploit all the market advantages associated with that name. In contrast, sole traders and partnerships have no such formal protection. A company may also be in a position to benefit from access to government grants, borrowing in the capital market, and gaining a degree of credibility with suppliers. Finally, there may also be taxation advantages that apply uniquely to incorporated businesses.

The drawbacks of forming a company are the necessary, and often costly, formalities that must be undertaken to ensure that it meets all legal requirements. In addition, companies are required by law to disclose financial information by way of annual accounts. This may be sufficient cause for some firms to remain as sole ownerships or partnerships.

Sam Walton

Sam Walton began as a franchisee of Ben Franklin five-and-ten stores. He noticed, however, that the trend in 1950s America was moving toward the discount store rather than the one-price store. He decided to follow his instinct and invest in a new venture, and so Wal-Mart was born.

Born: 1918, Kingfisher, Oklahoma
Importance: Developed the discount-store concept
Died: 1992, Little Rock, Arkansas

In 1940, Sam Walton joined the retailer J. C. Penny in Iowa as a trainee. He was impressed by Penny's commitment to the welfare of its employees—an approach he was to follow. In 1945, he opened his first store in Arkansas, under the Ben Franklin franchise. Within 15 years he was running nine stores across three states and had accumulated a wealth of knowledge and experience.

By the early 1960s, aware of the success of discount stores like Kmart, Walton and his brother opened their own discount store in Arkansas. The traditional view at the time was that discount stores were not suited to small towns and country communities. However, on the basis of his retailing experience, his ambition, and his near-exhaustive research of markets in the East, Walton felt that the strategy would succeed.

Walton's retailing success was built on tried-and-tested retail methods. As well as attractive prices, he ensured that shelves were constantly restocked, and that stores enjoyed a central location and remained open for long hours to attract as wide a range of customers as possible. By buying from low-priced suppliers and exploiting his buying power to the full, he was able to pass cost savings on to his customers by charging lower prices. In time, he would bypass the wholesalers altogether and deal directly with the manufacturers.

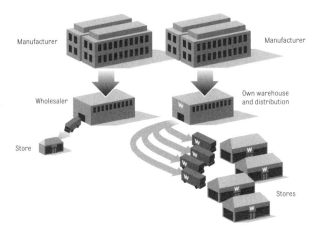

Above: Small stores usually buy their produce from wholesalers rather than manufacturers. The extra costs incurred by using a middleman are off-set by the savings the store makes on transportation and storage costs.

Larger firms can cut out the wholesaler because at high volumes of produce, economies of scale in storage and transport make paying a middleman unnecessary.

Walton initially concentrated on the South and Midwest, avoiding direct competition with large chain and department stores in the Northeast. His rivals were local chains and independent stores that dotted rural areas. When he did move close to a densely populated area, he would usually locate at the periphery. Because his stores were mostly in small towns, they had to serve the community in more ways than simply supplying goods. Wal-Mart therefore became involved in local community activities and promoted local causes. Not until the 1980s, when he felt sufficiently confident to launch the chain nationally, did Wal–Mart enter urban centers. By the time of Walton's death in 1992, there were more than 2,000 Wal-Mart stores.

Richard Branson

Richard Branson possesses a voracious appetite for new and exciting ventures, especially in markets dominated by a few powerful companies. Airlines, books, telecommunications, credit cards, holidays, fitness clubs, and space travel all sport the famous red Virgin logo. His distinctive risk taking, business success, and flamboyant personality have made him a British folk hero.

Born: 1950, Shamley Green, England
Importance: Exploited a successful brand in many diverse businesses

Although the young Branson had some business successes early in life, his breakthrough came with music retailer Virgin Megastore and its associated label, Virgin Records. One of the first Virgin records was Mike Oldfield's *Tubular Bells*—a phenomenal hit that sold 13 million copies. Despite his image, Branson was no laid-back music entrepreneur. His negotiations revealed a shrewd ability to extract favorable terms from his performers. He signed many of them to long contracts and ensured he had world rights to their output. In the mid-1970s, following successful record sales of key performers (including the Sex Pistols and Phil Collins), the business expanded and the label was launched in the United States.

In 1984, against sound advice, Branson took a gamble that was to propel his business into the big league: the launch of Virgin Atlantic Airways, initially offering services from London to New York and, subsequently, to Los Angeles and Tokyo. The new company promised a better, less stuffy service than the traditional, domineering giants like British Airways. Branson's publicity stunts, including powerboats and hot-air balloons, were a clever marketing ploy: he and his Virgin logo became a regular feature in the media.

With the success of the new business, Branson went public. Within a few years, however, he had bought the company back, keen to invest his profits in new ventures rather than having to pay dividends to shareholders. He plowed money into all sorts of activities and, sometimes to the exasperation of colleagues, there seemed little business reason for his acquisitions. It was hard to predict what Branson might turn to next.

Following the sale of his music business to EMI in 1992, Branson was able to make further investments in his airline and to offer a better and more competitive service. After winning a legal battle with British Airways, his popularity rose. Over the next decade Virgin diversified into cola, vodka, rail, insurance, telecommunications, and the Internet. However, by 2002, some of the businesses were sold and Branson was forced to concentrate on core activities. Undaunted, and with his characteristic grin, Branson will surely continue to seek new opportunities.

"Business opportunities are like buses, there's always another one coming."

Richard Branson

Two main factors have aided Branson's success. First, he focuses his activities on those industries where customers are badly served and develops marketing strategies that offer the same products in new and better ways. Second, he has personally become linked to the Virgin brand. His casual dress, beard, informality, and general nonconformity are seen by his customers as authentic, in the face of the corporate image of his rivals. The Virgin brand remains eternally popular across different industries because it echoes its owner's characteristics.

Phineas Taylor Barnum

For 60 years, Phineas Taylor Barnum gave 19th-century American audiences exhibitions and shows that managed to create both credulity and incredulity at the same time. Not only was he a great showman, but he was also an impresario who mastered the art of shameless and continuous promotion essential to a successful business.

Born: 1810, Bethel, Connecticut
Importance: An innovator in the promotion of mass amusement
Died: 1891, Bridgeport, Connecticut

Even at an early age, Barnum proved to be a good salesman, selling lottery tickets and organizing the management of a general store. At the age of 25, he acquired the services of one Joice Heth, who claimed to be 161 years old and to have been George Washington's nurse. With shameless audacity, Barnum promoted her with a flyer that read, "Unquestionably the most astonishing and interesting curiosity." The public was intrigued and flocked to view the spectacle in New York, making Barnum $1,500 a week—an unprecedented sum for a show of that nature.

In subsequent years he acquired a museum to which he added many thousands of additional exhibits from around the world, though not all were as genuine as was claimed. "Barnum's American Museum" on Broadway in New York was a huge success and the most visited exhibition in mid-19th-century America. He also acquired the "Feejee mermaid," billed, outrageously, as an embalmed mermaid, and promoted Charles Stratton, a famous midget, as "General Tom Thumb." In 1850, Barnum introduced the opera star Jenny Lind as the "Swedish Nightingale," who became a great success.

At the age of 60, Barnum organized a traveling museum, menagerie, and circus, which he named "The Greatest Show on

Left: Barnum's great skill was to inspire wonder and curiosity in his audience. Jumbo the Elephant was the first international animal celebrity, and the Feejee mermaid is now widely suspected to have been the torso of a monkey stitched to the tail of a large fish. Once Barnum's promotional magic had done its work, they became fantastical creatures that thousands paid to visit.

Earth." In time, the show traveled the country by rail, covered 5 acres (2 hectares) of ground when set up, and had room to seat 10,000 people. The show made $400,000 in its first year. Even as his career was coming to a close, Barnum was still able to create a spectacle. In 1882, he purchased Jumbo, an elephant from the London Zoo, as a stunt to publicize his show in New York. Britain was outraged. Newspapers, politicians, and people of influence protested. Britain went Jumbo crazy, with Jumbo hats, ties, fans, and cigars finding a ready market. The resulting fuss, almost certainly engineered by Barnum, reached America and most of New York came out to witness the arrival of Jumbo, the "Towering Monarch." The word "jumbo" is still often used synonymously for "elephant."

Barnum's success undoubtedly lay in his skill to capture the imagination of the public through his advertising. Early on in his life he realized the great power of publicity. In the first year of running his museum in New York, he spent all his profits on further promoting the business to sustain its long run of success.

Walt Disney

Walt Disney created the world-famous cartoon icon Mickey Mouse. As a filmmaker, Disney was nominated for 47 Academy Awards over his lifetime. On the back of the success of feature-length cartoons and films, he developed a theme park and, eventually, a worldwide multimedia company. Above all, he used his name as a brand to convey an image of wholesome, family entertainment.

Born: 1901, Chicago, Illinois
Importance: Filmmaker and entrepreneur
Died: 1966, Los Angeles, California

At the age of 18, having spent a year abroad in France with the army, Disney returned to America to begin a career in a Kansas City advertising agency, drawing cartoons. It was here that he moved into the art of animated film. In 1923, he left for Hollywood and, together with his brother Roy, raised sufficient funds to shoot a series of short films that combined live action with animated cartoons. The resulting series, the *Alice Comedies*, continued to be produced until 1927, when it became clear that Disney's animated characters were more popular than the real life stars of the show.

Disney was always at the forefront of technological innovation in picture production. When Mickey Mouse was created, in 1928, Disney combined animation with sound synchronization—a new technology in filmmaking. By the early 1930s, Disney cartoons were being produced in color and, in 1937, he pioneered the "multiplane camera technique," which allowed animators to reuse backgrounds or foregrounds that were not subject to action, thus saving production time.

Later that same year, Disney produced his first feature length animated film, *Snow White and the Seven Dwarfs*, at a cost of $1.5 million. This was an unprecedented amount for an animation in the motion-picture industry. The film was a great success and was followed with *Pinocchio*, *Fantasia*, and *Bambi*. The Disney studio in Burbank grew dramatically, eventually employing over 1,000 people, mostly animators and technical staff. Disney always strove for technical excellence and was reluctant to cut corners; as such, production costs were high. For example, he invested over $100,000 in training programs for dozens of young animators. The return from this investment was modest, however, since Disney picked only a few of the very best animators to work for him.

After the war, Disney turned to television and his magic worked there as well. *The Mickey Mouse Club*, *Zorro*, and *The Wonderful World of Disney* were just a few of the program successes. In 1955, he expanded into the business of amusement parks—now known as "theme parks." Disneyland in Anaheim, California, was designed to appeal to both adults and children, and by the time of his death, the park had been visited by close to seven million people. After his death similar parks were opened in Orlando, Florida, Tokyo, Japan, and Paris, France.

> "I never called my work an 'art.' It's part of show business, the business of building entertainment."
>
> Walt Disney

Disney is unique in the sense that probably no other single person has made such a terrific cultural impact in both America and the rest of the world. In business terms, he created and fiercely defended a reputation as a family-friendly brand that endures to this day.

Risk

Risk is usually defined as the uncertainty of an outcome or an event. It can refer either to a negative threat or to a positive opportunity for a company—taking a risk that pays off brings a competitive advantage over risk-averse rivals. However, given the potential for significant losses as well as gains, it is important that risks are assessed accurately by calculating the probability of an outcome as well as its impact on a business. The theory behind these assessments remains a major exercise for business analysts and academics.

All businesses face risks by operating in an environment of inherent uncertainties—the free market puts any economic activity at the mercy of supply and demand. As a consequence, all businesses must have a system in place for managing such outcomes. This typically involves the identification of all potential risks, determining as accurately as possible the chances of their taking place and their likely impact on the enterprise, and then developing an adequate, measured response to cope with such events if and when they occur.

Risks stem from a number of different areas. *Strategic* risks cover uncertainties that relate to the market, such as a fall in demand, a failure of new product development, or the entry of new rivals. *Financial* risks relate to changes in cost and revenue that are not directly linked to the market. These might include bad debts or an increase in the interest payments due on loans. *Operational* risks cover the dangers of a breakdown of production and distribution functions, such as failure of factory machinery or the loss of key staff. Finally, *compliance* risks relate to a company's ability to meet legal and regulatory requirements. Failure to do so can result in the forced closure of the business or the threat of legal action. More general risks would include natural disasters and political instability in foreign markets.

Once risks have been identified, it is important for a business to assess their likelihood and their impact or significance. A business can then rank or prioritize the risks it faces. This ranking allows resources to focus on the most important areas of risk, those that have the greatest potential impact on the success of a company's objectives. Estimating risk can be achieved on a basic level, simply by estimating whether outcomes are of low, moderate, or high probability. At a more sophisticated level, risks can be assessed by the application of actuarial science.

The final stage is the development of systems, or policies, for managing risk. The first approach is simply to *accept* the risk. This usually means that the costs of dealing with the risk outweigh the costs of the risk itself. Risks that cannot be avoided or transferred fall into this category of "self-insurance." The second strategy is to *transfer* the risk. This is normally carried out by buying an insurance policy. Risk can also be transferred by contractual agreement. (For example, a buyer may agree to meet all the costs of production of a supplying firm.) The third is to *reduce* the risk by making various investments, such as buying better, more expensive machinery with a lower probability of a breakdown. The final approach is to *avoid* the risk. This means that an activity or investment is not undertaken because the risks are considered too high. The problem with such an approach is that profitable opportunities sometimes have to be forgone.

Anita Roddick

As a means of supporting herself and her two daughters while her husband was away on an expedition, Anita Roddick opened a shop. In 1976, with little background in business and retailing, but with a wealth of experience from her travels around the world, Roddick launched The Body Shop, with its unique focus on ethical products. The business expanded to around 2,000 stores, serving 70 million people in 50 different countries.

Born: 1942, Littlehampton, England
Importance: Developed a multinational retail business combining principles with profits
Died: 2007, Chichester, England

Roddick's first shop, in Brighton, England, began with a few simple ideas. Based on her own experience, she noticed how difficult it was for travelers to buy small bath products. Her first range of 15 natural cosmetics were packaged in small, recyclable bottles with minimum labeling in order to keep costs down. Her choice of green for her uniforms was to hide damp spots rather than to make a grand statement about green issues. Her almost instant success allowed her to open a second shop and then, together with her husband, to sell the idea to other investors as a franchise operation. They charged no start-up fee, but Roddick would interview each franchisee to ensure he or she shared the same philosophy. She applied the same principle when hiring employees, to ensure that her sales staff would support the company's greater aims in their work.

The philosophy behind The Body Shop was different from that of other perfume and cosmetic companies in that its objective was to make profits with principles based on notions of social and environmental responsibility. As her publicity stated, the "two for one" at her shops meant a bar of soap and justice.

The shopping experience in The Body Shop was developed around creating an environment that empowered the customer. On entering a shop people were not "jumped on" by sales staff; there were no glamorous pictures of models; products were labeled with full information; and brochures and literature covering relevant issues were available for those customers who might be interested.

The business was rarely advertised in the conventional sense. Instead, the message spread indirectly in two ways. First, through word of mouth from customers satisfied with the quality and service. Second, through clever use of the media, the business became associated with various campaigns. The early success of The Body Shop in Brighton owed much to Roddick leaking a story to the local press about the neighboring funeral directors who were upset by the name

> "We turned all the shops into action stations to educate the public on certain issues such as human rights."
> Anita Roddick

of the shop. Over the years, The Body Shop has supported a number of campaigns, such as Save-the-Whale, Save the Brazilian Rainforest, and Fair Trade. They have also supported organizations including Friends of the Earth and Amnesty.

From what was once considered a "hippy" outlet, the business has developed into a successful multinational retail organization. Controversially, in 2006, Roddick sold the business to L'Oréal, which is partly owned by Nestlé. This proved contentious: not only was L'Oréal allegedly involved in animal testing but Nestlé had also been subject to a boycott because of the sale of its infant milk to mothers in the Third World.

Coco Chanel

Coco Chanel was an intuitive and influential designer. Her signature creation was the "little black dress," as well as jersey dresses and gray pullovers. Her style suggested practical simplicity, while the high price implied a degree of exclusivity and elegance. After World War II, she became one of the most imitated designers, as her business expanded and diversified into handbags, textiles, and the famous perfume Chanel No. 5.

Born: 1883, Saumur, France
Importance: Among the world's best-known couturiers
Died: 1971, Paris, France

Chanel started working in the early part of the 20th century as a chanteuse in cafés and concert halls, where she picked up the name "Coco." By 1910, with the support of wealthy lovers, she opened a millinery store in Paris and, soon after, in Biarritz and Deauville.

Chanel pioneered the use of jersey as a fashion fabric. Until the 1920s, it had been used to produce underwear. Wool jersey produced a softer, lighter fabric that created fluid lines complementing the body's natural shape. Chanel's loose-fitting garments freed women from the more traditional formal clothes and corsets that had "shaped" the woman's body up to now. Her designs often came from male fashion, and she frequently took inspiration from riding breeches, wide-bottomed trousers, blazers, and sweaters. Her most famous creations were the "little black dress" and the "Chanel suit," which consisted of a cardigan-style jacket, simple skirt, and blouse. She was also credited with encouraging shorter skirts and short hair.

The product most associated with Chanel is her perfume, developed and launched in 1922. It was referred to as No. 5 simply because it was the fifth formula to be tested. It was the first perfume to be sold across the world, and is still an extremely well known and profitable product to this day, with a bottle being sold every 30 seconds. Unfortunately, Chanel made relatively little money from the product as most of the revenue went to a partner.

> "Fashion fades, only style remains the same."
> Coco Chanel

Following a self-imposed exile in Switzerland during World War II, Chanel returned to France in 1954 to reopen her business, which had been closed since 1939. She pioneered the "New Look," again focusing on a soft, casual, and relaxed style. The Chanel style quickly gained in popularity, particularly in the United States, and business boomed.

Chanel was one of the first couturiers to recognize that the fashion industry had changed. Rather than focusing on an exclusive product tailored to the elite, she saw that the future lay in marketing a fashionable brand to less affluent, but more numerous, buyers of ready-to-wear clothing. Chanel built up contacts with American prêt à porter manufacturers, allowing Chanel products to be mass-produced for sale at a reasonable price. This successful strategy was copied decades later by many other fashion houses such as Calvin Klein, Donna Karan, and Versace.

The House of Chanel continues to this day, currently under the direction of Karl Lagerfeld, who has updated the classic, uncomplicated style to appeal to a modern market.

Mary Kay Ash

A successful saleswoman, Mary Kay Ash set up her own direct-selling company, Mary Kay Cosmetics, in Dallas. Thanks to her leadership and innovative organization, the business grew dramatically. Starting with just nine sales staff, the business now has over one million employees worldwide.

Born: 1918, Hot Wells, Texas
Importance: Developed a
unique business approach
Died: 2001, Dallas, Texas

With a background in direct selling, Mary Ash found employment with Stanley Home Products in 1939. Although she was one of the top sales directors, she was consistently refused the pay raises and promotions enjoyed by her male colleagues. In 1953, she left the business for another direct-selling company in St. Louis, but, again, her success was not rewarded so she retired in 1963 and decided to write a book about her experiences. As the book took form, Ash realized that she had been writing a business plan for her dream company.

In 1963, with the help of her son, Ash invested $5,000 in skin-care cream and a cosmetics company to sell it. The company was built around "party plan" direct selling: "beauty consultants" bought the product from Ash and organized parties in people's homes to sell it. Each consultant's income was based on their sales of the skin-care product—bought at 50 percent of the retail price—plus a generous bonus for every new "beauty consultant" they introduced to the business. Novice consultants received training and advice on effective direct selling.

The key strategies in selling the product were strict. The company manufactured a limited line of products to ensure the sales force had a good knowledge of them. The focus at the parties was first to teach customers about skin care, and only later

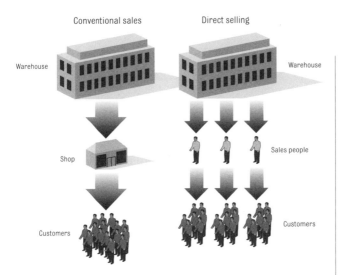

Conventional sales

Direct selling

Warehouse

Warehouse

Shop

Sales people

Customers

Customers

Above: In conventional sales, goods from the warehouse reach individual customers through a store. In direct selling, the salesperson buys goods from the warehouse and sells them on a personal basis to parties of six customers at a time. The savings on shop premises and upkeep can be put towards cultivating a highly trained, skilled, and motivated sales force.

to sell the product. Company policy restricted each party to six women, guaranteeing a more personal service. Having a limited line of products meant that consultants could carry all stock and therefore make immediate delivery, exploiting the impulse buy. In addition, the business did not sell stock to its consultants on credit, which ensured that they did not overextend themselves. Finally, it was company policy that remuneration was more generous than in other, similar, firms. Ash believed in providing real incentives for her workforce, famously giving her top salespeople pink Cadillacs.

Branding

A successful brand is an easily identifiable product or service, augmented by an array of unique and relevant values added to their basic material value, which meet the desires of the consumer. The brand links these values to a particular supplier who then enjoys exclusive rights to its use for an unlimited period of time.

Branding is an important strategy, used both to alert the market to a company's products and to allow the market to *differentiate* between such products and those offered by competitors. A successful brand will not only confer superior profits and increased market share but will also generate long-term competitive advantages by establishing both a good reputation and a strong connection in the minds of consumers between the product or service and the particular company.

A brand is created by the use of a distinctive name (Kodak), packaging (Coca-Cola), symbol (Lacoste), design (Burberry), or any combination of these. The advantage of creating a distinct identity, or value, is that it allows consumers to associate quality, reliability, and price with a given product. A brand is, in effect, a company's promise to deliver these additional attributes and thus reduce the consumer's anxiety that he or she may be making the wrong choice.

All products and services offer fundamental benefits: a watch tells you the time, a restaurant satisfies your hunger, and a car gets you where you want to go. A brand, however, will add to these benefits by generating further advantages. A branded watch may suggest a degree of exclusivity, a branded restaurant a perception of value for money, and a branded car may carry the suggestion of reliability or social status. A successful brand is thus defined as one that contributes extra value to the core benefits of a product. This additional value is often referred to as *brand equity*.

Strong brand equity can generate a number of advantages for a firm. First, it can increase net revenue by allowing the firm to charge a premium price above that of a generic substitute and by reducing future promotional costs. In addition, consumers remain loyal for longer periods of time and thus allow for a more stable flow of income. Second, a strong brand will permit a company greater bargaining power with distributors and retailers, since it knows that consumers will expect outlets to stock the brand. Third, brand equity associated with one product can also be seen as an asset to be exploited elsewhere. Thus the firm may wish to expand the brand to cover a wider range of products. This is referred to as *brand extension*. If a firm is unwilling to exploit the financial advantages of a successful brand itself, it may decide to lease or sell it to other firms operating in unrelated markets. Fourth, a strong brand may deter potential entrants into a market. The entrant is faced not only with the investment of developing a new brand but also with the additional marketing cost of having to lure existing loyal customers away from the incumbent brands.

Brands also help to promote distributional efficiencies. When a consumer purchases a branded product, the expectation is of a minimum standard of quality and value. There is no need to carry out individual search costs to ascertain the full set of characteristics of the product, which would be the case if no branding existed. Successful branding allows consumers to reward producers with repeat purchases.

J. P. Morgan

In his time, J. P. Morgan was the most important banker in the United States. He was able to raise sufficient funds to invest in the newly expanding railroad industry, as well as managing the massive national debt incurred as a result of the Civil War. In 1907, he averted a crisis in the banking system by enlisting the help of other bankers to avoid a financial panic.

Born: 1837, Hartford, Connecticut
Importance: Banker and financier of major industrial companies
Died: 1913, Rome, Italy

In 1871, J. P. Morgan became a partner in his father's company, Drexel, Morgan, & Co., where he proved to be an outstanding banker, adding much to his personal fortune. Using his business knowledge and contacts in Europe, Morgan specialized in selling American stock—notably U.S. Government bonds—to European investors. The company also became an important player in the refinancing of the large U.S. debt caused by the Civil War. By 1895, he had reorganized the company as J. P. Morgan & Co., regarded by most as a financial and investment giant.

An important aspect of Morgan's activities was the financing of major industrial enterprises. His loans enabled mergers, acquisitions, and investments that gave rise to large trusts—an important feature of American industry in the late 19th century. Initially his main interest was selling railroad stock, especially to European investors. Morgan often demanded that, in return for the selling of the stock, he maintained a degree of control in the railroad. As a consequence, he frequently "Morganized" the business by introducing his own workers, fresh ideas, and new strategies. For a time he even attempted to organize railroad cartels, in order to minimize the effect of ruinous competition.

In the merger boom of the early 1900s, Morgan was midwife to some of the great organizations that remain to this day. For example, he organized and financed the merger of Edison General Electric and Thompson-Houston Electric to form the electrical equipment manufacturer General Electric. He also created International Merchant Marine (an Atlantic shipping line) and International Harvester (manufacturing agricultural equipment).

Having financed the creation of Federal Steel, he then merged it with Carnegie Steel to form the massive U.S. Steel Corporation (see pages 36–37). Morgan's strategy was to achieve greater economies of scale by reducing transport costs and improving distribution. The larger business was also in a position to extend its power into other industries through vertical integration, by developing new products such

> "Money equals business which equals power, all of which come from character and trust."
>
> J. P. Morgan

as bridges, ships, rails, railroad carriages, wires, and nails. Furthermore, the size of the corporation allowed it to challenge steel companies in Britain and Europe.

Morgan's financial power was so immense that he was even able to steady the U.S. economy when it was threatened with a financial panic in 1907. He organized a pool among bankers to bail out failing banks, so preventing potential "run-on banks." His unequaled power in investment banking worried politicians, which led to various Senate investigations and, eventually, the creation of the Federal Reserve as the official guarantor of the banking system.

John D. Rockefeller

John D. Rockefeller dominated the oil industry in the United States at the turn of the 20th century. Rockefeller realized from his early experiences that, for an oil company to be successful, it had to be large in order to benefit from potential economies of scale.

Born: 1839, Richmond, New York
Importance: Founder of Standard Oil and involved in many corporate financial deals
Died: 1937, Ormond Beach, Florida

Rockefeller was brought up in Cleveland, Ohio, and in 1855 found employment as an accountant in a small transportation company. Although still in his teens, he soon learnt enough about the business to trade on his own. In 1863, he moved into oil refining. Together with a new partner, Samuel Andrews, who had experience of the oil industry, he set up Rockefeller & Andrews in 1865, when he was only 24. The company profited dramatically from technical improvements, the ability to exploit economies of large scale, and vertical integration. In 1870, having borrowed additional finances and attracted new partners, the company became the Standard Oil Company.

Rockefeller realized that the oil-refining industry was poorly structured. Entry costs into extracting and refining were low, and there were many small competing firms. In order to survive, these firms drove prices down to the detriment of the larger, better managed firms. The solution was to get rid of the competition.

In late 1871, Rockefeller launched a strategy to take over most of his rivals in Cleveland. He targeted the strongest first to avoid forcing the takeover price too high as competitors got wind of the strategy. He offered the owners either stock in Standard Oil or cash. Although it was a popular view that these owners had been treated unfairly with threats of a price war, evidence shows that the prices paid were fair. Faced with a dominant low-cost

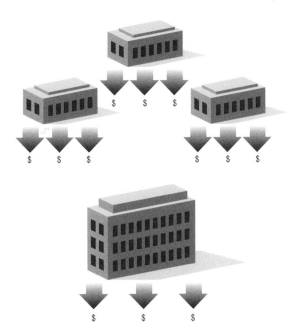

Above: The total operating costs for three refineries each producing 100,000 barrels of oil per day will be greater than those for one refinery producing 300,000 barrels per day. By reducing the number of refineries and making sure each one operated as efficiently as possible, Rockefeller was able to bring down the costs of production and dominate the market.

producer, there really was little future for the medium-sized businesses. By 1872, Rockefeller controlled 22 of Cleveland's 26 oil companies. The inefficient plants were dismantled and the efficient ones were incorporated into the Standard Oil empire.

The company prospered and in 1882 it was consolidated into the Standard Oil Trust. It generated great efficiencies in production and distribution, leading to an astonishing 80 percent fall in retail prices.

Financial Geniuses

Jay Gould

It was claimed that Jay Gould was the first of the robber barons, who operated in financial and industrial markets with little regard to ethical behavior. There was little he wouldn't consider to further his ambitions. The issuing of watered stock, attempts to corner the gold market, strikebreaking, and bribery are just a few of the famous examples of the strategies he used.

Born: 1836, Roxbury, New York
Importance: Financier and speculator active chiefly in the railroad industry
Died: 1892, New York

Although Gould had invested in a tannery in Pennsylvania and later became a leather merchant in New York, it was Wall Street that attracted him most, with its endless opportunities for trading and speculating. It didn't take Gould long to become an expert in the complicated workings of the markets and he was soon making large returns from his ventures, mostly specializing in railroad stock.

In 1867, Gould was invited to join the board of the financially troubled Erie Railroad and soon came across a potent rival in Cornelius Vanderbilt (see pages 38–39). Vanderbilt had long wanted to own the Erie and, in 1868, started to buy its stock. Gould and his directors responded by illegally converting company bonds into 100,000 new shares. Vanderbilt responded with legal action, only to see Gould bribe the New York State legislators to legalize the issue. Vanderbilt knew he was beaten and accepted a $1 million settlement, leaving the Erie to Gould. On the promise of grandiose investment plans, Gould increased Erie's capital debt and then sold its stock

"...a spider (who) spun huge webs, in corners and in the dark."

Henry Adams

short, allowing him to make vast profits before its eventual demise in 1875.

Another well-documented Gould venture was his attempt to manipulate the price of gold so as to weaken the dollar. This would increase foreign demand for American wheat, and thus increase demand for his wheat-carrying railroad. In 1869 he began to buy gold on the free market, hoping that the U.S. Treasury would not intervene by selling its own stock to stabilize the market price. When the price of gold had risen to $160, the treasury was forced to intervene by selling gold, and the price fell to $135 causing many to lose substantial sums. Gould made only a modest return on the venture, and subsequent lawsuits resulted in the loss of his reputation.

Undaunted by the financial scandal, Gould turned his interests toward the acquisition of western railroad companies as well as the addition of the profitable Manhattan Elevated Railroad and Western Union Telegraph. His strategy was to buy companies at a low price in times of depression and sell some of them when the market recovered. In this way he made substantial capital gains and added to his fortune. By the 1880s he owned 15 percent of all rail mileage in the United States. Regardless of the negative publicity, Gould achieved a remarkable feat by providing an integrated national rail and communications network, as well as developing Western Union as a dominant force in America's telegraph industry.

Watered stock:
Stock with an artificially inflated value. The term comes from the practice of bloating cattle with water just before auction to increase their weight and boost their sale price. In market terms, a company's stock is said to be watered if the value of the stock sold exceeds the true value of the company.

Company Stock

Stock is the term for capital that has been raised by a corporation in return for a share in the ownership of that company. A stockholding not only confers an ownership right, but also a proportionate claim on the profits and, in the event of liquidation, on the assets of the company.

A company can issue any number of shares up to an authorized number. These shares can be traded at stock exchanges, or bought and sold privately, at prices determined by the interaction of supply and demand in the market. Thus, if demand for shares is high—in other words if the stock is sufficiently popular that there are more buyers than sellers—prices rise, to ration the available supply. If demand is low, prices fall to encourage otherwise reluctant investors. Stock exchanges provide a ready market for such transactions, allowing shareholders to buy and sell shares at their convenience. The ability to "liquidate" shares at any time—convert them back into cash by selling them on the stock market—is a great attraction to investors.

Shareholders have a right to participate in the distribution of profits and assets of the company in proportion to their shareholdings, traditionally through the exercise of their votes at the Annual General Meeting (AGM). The degree of power they wield is largely dependent on the level of share concentrations held by individuals and other companies. The lower the level of concentrated ownership—i.e., the more evenly ownership of stock is spread between investors—the more difficult it is to organize a serious challenge to the board of directors at an AGM. In most cases the board will have sufficient proxy votes from the non-attending shareholders to outvote any challenge to their company policy from the floor.

Although shareholders have a claim on the profits or dividends of a company, this claim is unsecured, which means that they are the last to be paid in the event of bankruptcy. The assets of a company pay off all other creditors and there may be little left for the holders of equity stock. If there is a serious danger of a company failing, share prices may fall close to zero as investors attempt to sell off their stock and cut their losses.

There are some other dangers of holding shares. The value of shares is more volatile than that of other types of investment. Prices fluctuate from day to day, influenced by the activities of large buyers and sellers, such as the institutional investors (banks, insurance companies, retirement funds, hedge funds, etc.), as well as changes in the wider economy and political environment. The market can be subject to waves of pessimism and optimism, both of which can seem at times to defy rational thought. For this reason, many investors in ordinary shares will diversify their holdings to reduce the risk of "gambler's ruin" and include many shares drawn from a wide variety of industries and offsetting activities. In addition, investors also diversify their portfolios with the inclusion of other securities such as bonds and gilt-edged (government) stock.

The term "stock" as specifying ownership rights in a company is one used in the United States, whereas the UK and Australia use the word "share." In the UK, "stocks" refer to a much wider set of marketable securities. "Ordinary shares" (as opposed to preference shares) are often called "equities," as they represent the "equity" of the company. This is the value of the company after all creditor claims have been met.

The Rothschild Dynasty

The paterfamilias of the Rothschild dynasty was Mayer Amschel Rothschild (1773–1812). Having attracted many rich and powerful clients to his Frankfurt finance house, storing gold bullion and issuing loans, his business prospered and he taught his five sons the essentials of banking practice. He then sent them to major financial centers in Europe, where they were able to expand the business on an international scale unprecedented at the time.

Born: Mayer Amschel Rothschild 1773, Frankfurt am-Main, Germany
Importance: Developed international banking to serve world governments and industries
Died: Mayer Amschel Rothschild 1812, Frankfurt-am-Main, Germany

Of the five sons, Nathan was sent to London and James went to Paris. Two others went to Vienna and Naples, and the fifth stayed back with Amschel in Frankfurt. The London and Paris enterprises prospered most, primarily owing to the friendly competition that existed between the two "houses." As a result, the Rothschilds were able to finance both the British and French participation during the Napoleonic Wars in the first quarter of the 19th century.

On balance, however, it was Nathan in London who was the more successful in the world of finance and business. It is claimed that he increased the family's fortune greatly by speculating on the outcome of the Battle of Waterloo in 1815, correctly predicting Napoleon's defeat. With his sophisticated and speedy communications network of agents in Europe, Nathan was able to get news of the outcome of the battle before most of the population of London. He then spread rumors of a French victory to depress stock market prices, so that he could buy shares cheaply and sell them at a profit when the news of the victory eventually reached the general public.

Nathan and his brother were responsible for the creation of modern European banking and, in particular, the development of the international bond market. A

> "Give me control of a nation's money and I care not who makes the laws."
>
> Mayer Amschel Rothschild

government bond allowed investors to buy government debt at fixed interest rates. This was popular with governments, who could now raise large sums of money to finance wars and public works. Since this stock could be traded, speculators could take "positions" on the future value of the stock. As volumes in the bonds market increased, the Rothschilds—as underwriters—made vast fortunes, which they invested heavily into mining, rail, and steel companies around the world. Nathan's bank became so powerful that he was even able to come to the aid of the Bank of England when it faced a run on gold.

In recent times, the company has become more focused on its activities as a merchant bank, arranging acquisitions and mergers and issuing company stock. It is now ranked as the fourth largest in Europe and ninth in the world for advising firms on restructuring. One criticism of the company was its failure to exploit opportunities in the United States during the 19th century, preferring to stay close to its core European activities.

An important factor in the continuing success of the banking family through the 19th and 20th centuries has been family unity. Since marriage outside the extended family was frowned upon, a very tight-knit family unit developed, creating a unity that resulted in the nominally independent houses being run de facto as one organization.

Warren Buffett

Warren Buffett is chairman of holding company Berkshire
Hathaway, which he bought in 1965. He used the company's cash
to acquire stocks and shares in many companies, including
Coca-Cola, Gillette, and American Express. Buffett's investments
have proved a phenomenal success, making him one
of the richest men in the world.

Born: 1930, Omaha,
Nebraska
Importance: Perhaps the
world's greatest and most
successful stock market
investor

It was at the Graduate School of Business at
Columbia University, New York, that Buffett met the
man who was to have a profound effect on his life.
Benjamin Graham had written a book on securities,
in which his theory of "value investing" suggested
that investors should buy stock that was underpriced
in relation to the value of the assets tied up in a
company. Graham assumed that, in time, the market would
realize the undervaluation and prices would rise, thus making a
profit for the investor. This implied that the investor should do a
lot of research to estimate accurately the value of all the assets
before buying stock. Buffett was ideally suited to this task; in later
years he claimed that he owed his success, in part, to reading
thousands of corporate annual reports.

Buffett worked for Graham in New York for a time but left in
1956 to set up the Buffett Partnership, an investment business, in
Omaha. Over the following 13 years, the partnership's initial
capital of $100,000 rose to a value of over $100 million. In 1965,
Buffett bought Berkshire Hathaway, a New England textile
company, and dissolved the Buffett Partnership in 1969 to focus
on this new purchase. Although he was forced to close the
manufacturing business in the early 1980s, the company has
survived as a holding company for his many profitable acquisitions.

Left: Markets with differentiated products tend to be dominated by one or two major brands. Entry into these markets by a new brand is often very difficult, as the existing brand is hard to unseat. By buying into dominant brands, Buffett gave his new business ventures the strongest possible start in the existing markets.

The targets for Buffett's investments tended to be insurance companies, which are cash rich thanks to regular payments from policies that may not have to pay out for many years, if at all. Buffett's strategy was to use this cash to buy businesses that formed the backbone of his investments. These tended to be companies with distinctive competitive advantages, such as a brand image—Coca-Cola, for example—as opposed to businesses that sold undifferentiated products. Entry barriers would be greater in markets characterized by differentiated products and so these companies were relatively free of potential competition. They were also typically very successful and generated yet more cash to expand Buffett's portfolio still further.

As the businesses and investments grew, so did Buffett's influence in shaping and brokering major events in the corporate world. In 1995, he arranged the $19 billion acquisition of Cap Cities/ABC by the Walt Disney Corporation to form a new media empire. So successful was Buffett in these ventures that $1,000 invested in Berkshire Hathaway in 1965 was worth $5 million in 2000. In 2006 Buffett made a promise to give 85 percent of his wealth, a staggering $35 billion, to charity.

Rupert Murdoch

From owning a small provincial newspaper in Australia, Murdoch managed to turn his company, the News Corporation, into one of the largest and most powerful media groups in the world, with a presence not only in newspapers and magazines, but also in television, film, and the Internet. Furthermore, Murdoch has exploited his power richly, not only in the business world, but also in the political arena.

Born: 1931, Melbourne, Australia
Importance: A diversified media owner with a unique global presence

When Murdoch left Oxford University in England, he spent a brief spell on the *Daily Express* newspaper, before returning to Australia to run his father's paper, the *Adelaide News*. Within a few years he began to acquire more publications, notably the *Sydney Daily Mirror*, which became the largest-selling paper in Australia. Circulation climbed as a result of its sensational and scandal-led stories.

In 1969, Murdoch turned his attention to the UK, buying the *News of the World* and later *The Sun*. The latter, once revamped, soon gained notoriety with its daily helpings of sex, crime, and scandal—a formula that proved extremely popular with the British public—and, as its circulation rose, it became the most profitable of Murdoch's titles. He also bought the British newspaper *The Times*, which like his *The Australian*, was aimed at a more serious market.

His early days in newspaper publishing in the UK are probably best remembered for his fight with the print unions over the adoption of a new technology in 1986. The unions had long resisted electronic typesetting, which allowed journalists to bypass the compositing rooms and submit copy direct to production. Murdoch moved his operations out of Fleet Street into Wapping, where he "locked out" the printers. After a bitter six months, it became clear that the unions had lost and the cost-reducing technology was subsequently widely adopted across the UK newspaper industry.

In the mid-1970s, Murdoch moved into the U.S. market with the purchase of the *National Star*, which he successfully transformed into an American version of *The Sun*. He then bought the *New York Post*, the *Boston Herald*, and the *Chicago Sun-Times*.

Murdoch's formula for success is no secret. He ensures that his newspapers appeal to popular tastes and are marketed in a positive, brash manner. He also keeps strict control over costs and is quick to adopt new ideas and technologies. He has received criticism for pushing political messages through his media products, which some believe he does in order to court the favor of those in power. The support of Murdoch-owned media for the governments of Tony Blair in Britain, and George W. Bush in the United States. has sparked controversy.

> "I don't run anything for respectability."
>
> Rupert Murdoch

In the 1980s, Murdoch moved into related fields of media management. He acquired Satellite TV in the UK and, to ensure a steady diet of films and sport for his Sky Channel, he bought the film company 20th Century Fox and television rights for showing English Premiership football. He also entered the American television market, having to become a U.S. citizen to do so. He has extensive interests in cable TV, book publishing, records, and a share in Reuters. The success of these ventures continues to make Murdoch a wealthy man.

Mergers and Acquisitions

A merger occurs when there is mutual agreement on the part of the management of two companies. An acquisition, or takeover, occurs when the management of one firm makes a direct offer to the shareholders of the other and is willing to pay a higher price for their shares than the prevailing stock market valuation. In practice, a clear distinction is not always possible.

There comes a time when many successful medium-sized firms consider further expansion to exploit potential economies of scale and scope and to make use of additional opportunities that a larger scale operation can often deliver. The essence of the strategy is to create a market value that is greater than the sum of the companies involved. We shall examine the benefits of both vertical and horizontal mergers.

Horizontal mergers occur when firms combine at the same stage of production—for example, two banks or two automobile manufacturers. There are a number of specific reasons why firms choose to merge. A horizontal merger may grant a firm a larger market share or the removal of a close rival. Either outcome may increase the resulting firm's ability to raise prices without having to worry about the reactions of rivals.

A common argument in favor of horizontal mergers is that the combined size of the two firms leads to economies of scale. Since efficiency gains can be achieved through a firm's own internal expansion, only *merger-specific gains* are relevant here. These involve the integration of specific, *hard-to-trade assets* owned by the merging firms. These gains are referred to as synergies. One example involves the *coordination of joint operation*: two firms linked by the joint management of a resource—such as an oil field—may face contractual and institutional problems leading to inefficiencies. A merger might lead to a reduction in such inefficiencies. Another example involves *the sharing of complementary skills*, where, for example, one firm may enjoy superior manufacturing skills, while the rival is better at distribution. Or perhaps one firm's patent can be fully and quickly exploited using the resources of a second firm.

Vertical mergers occur when two firms combine at different stages of production—for example a steel manufacturer acquiring coal mines. Reasons for such a merger tend to focus on the following issues: the technological advantages of linking successive stages of production; risk and uncertainty attached to the supply of materials or the distribution of a firm's finished product; the avoidance of government taxation and price controls; and, finally, a desire to secure market power.

The incentive to integrate vertically will exist where the market fails to work well (proves costly). In such cases the firm internalizes that particular market transaction by, for example, acquiring a supplying firm. It substitutes internal organization for external market exchange. The firm benefits from internal organization in three ways: incentives, controls, and inherent structural advantages. *Incentives* cover the advantages of being able to avoid costly and time-consuming bargaining with other producers at different stages of production. *Controls* imply that the firm can benefit from exerting more power over intrafirm activity as opposed to interfirm activity. *Structural advantages* may increase the economies of communication exchange. Therefore, staff within the organization share common training, experiences, and codes of practice, which ensures that the quality of the communications is improved.

Kun Hee Lee

As chief executive officer (CEO) of the Samsung Group, Kun Hee Lee was responsible, in the early 1990s, for a fundamental shift in the direction of the company. He recognized that the focus was on volume rather than quality and decided to "change everything."

By concentrating on better design and quality, Lee pushed Samsung Electronics into becoming a major force in world business.

Born: 1942, Uiryung, South Korea
Importance: Propelled Samsung Electronics into the world arena

Between 1977 and 1987, sales in the Samsung Group—at the time run by Kun Hee Lee's father Byung Chull Lee—rose from $1 billion to $24 billion, much of it attributed to Samsung Electronics. On his father's death, in 1987, Lee reorganized the group, placing more emphasis on training, motivation, and quality issues. Specifically, he invested in the electronics division, which was increasingly the most lucrative arm of the business. His desire was to make the company a dominant force in world markets, and particularly in the semiconductor business. To achieve this, he negotiated partnership deals with American and Japanese firms and acquired other firms such as Harris Microwave Semiconductors in 1993.

The result was an incredible twofold rise in sales between 1987 and 1992. However, Lee was not one to rest on his laurels. He increased his investments in research and development in order to maintain Samsung's position at the forefront of electronics technology, ahead of his competitors. He sold off various underperforming businesses, downsized others, and restructured the Samsung

"Change everything except your wife and kids."

Kun Hee Lee

Group into three distinct areas: electronics, engineering, and chemical processing.

Lee was also very keen to maintain the highest standards of quality. When, in 1995, it was reported in the media that he had, to his embarrassment, sent friends defective Samsung cell phones, he took drastic action. He arrived at the main plant at Gumi, south of Seoul, and forced the 2,000 employees to assemble outside wearing "quality first" headbands while witnessing the ritual destruction of the plant's entire stock. The cell phones now produced at the plant are built to the highest standard, and Lee and his executives currently aim to become the number one cell phone producer in the world.

Today, Samsung is a premier electronics company, dominating the world market in the production of memory chips, liquid crystal display (LCD) screens, and computer monitors. The company has also managed to overtake one-time rival Sony. With total assets close to $200 billion and employing 250,000 people worldwide in over 60 countries, Lee's company has achieved much in his tenure as CEO. Not least is the positive effect his measures have had on the economy of South Korea. Lee believes that the greatest assets a company can possess are creativity and design prowess. It is these competencies that determine a company's success. In striving for them, Lee developed a corporate culture that he sums up with the slogan "change myself first."

Quality control:
With increasingly expensive and complex products, and fiercely competitive markets, product safety and reliability is a high priority for all manufacturers. A wide range of quality control testing, using random samples and statistical analyses, is required to ensure that the proportion of faulty products is kept to a minimum.

Akio Morita

Akio Morita founded Tokyo Telecommunications with Masaru Ibuka in 1957. Initially they produced pocket-sized transistor radios. The company name soon changed to Sony and, over the next 40 years, went from strength to strength, generating a host of fresh and innovative products, many of which became synonymous with the brand name. By the time of his retirement in 1994, Morita's company was one of the largest producers of consumer electronics in the world.

Born: 1921, Nagoya, Japan
Importance: Founder of Sony, one of the first global corporations
Died: 1999, Tokyo, Japan

Morita grew up in a family that ran a successful sake brewery. It came as little surprise when, having attended university and spent time in the Japanese navy, he moved into business. He had studied physics, and in 1946, launched a company producing electronic equipment, primarily tape recorders. The major shareholders were relatives. In 1955, having bought the General Electric license to manufacture transistors, his business moved into the production of handheld transistor radios, the first such product in the world.

Unlike other Japanese firms that were producing goods for American companies (for example, Pentax for Honeywell and Sanyo for Sears), Morita's company was producing under its own name. The name "Sony" derived from the Latin word for sound (*sonus*), and Morita felt it would appeal to Western ears. To ensure success, he made certain that quality control lay at the forefront of company strategy. His efforts in product design and marketing ensured that "Made in Japan" would no longer imply cheap, shoddy copies, but products of the highest quality.

Morita's marketing skills combined well with Ibuka's technical leadership, and the company embarked on an ambitious strategy to identify potential new products and markets. Up to 10 percent of sales revenue was reinvested in research and development, and the business pursued lines of research free of any government or *keiretsu* (business alliance) help and support. The result was the introduction of innovatory products such as the Walkman, the Trinitron television, and compact discs.

The Sony Corporation of America was incorporated in 1971 and became the first Japanese company to produce television sets in the United States. By 1976, Morita had become chairman of the company. To complement its hardware, Sony moved into the software business of music and film. In 1987, it acquired CBS Records for $2 billion and, two years later, it bought Columbia Pictures for $3.5 billion.

Morita did make mistakes. In the early days of video, Sony backed Betamax as opposed to the Video Home System (VHS), which became the industry standard. The acquisition of Columbia Pictures also resulted in significant losses. Following Morita's death in 1994, Sony's dominance in the consumer electronics business was usurped by the adventurous Korean company Samsung (see pages 78–79). On balance however, the successes have more than outweighed these setbacks. Morita's legacy remains as the first entrepreneur to have developed a truly worldwide company with an instantly recognizable brand.

> "Don't be afraid to make a mistake. But make sure you don't make the same mistake twice."
>
> Akio Morita

Jack Welch

Jack Welch joined General Electric (GE) in 1960 and stayed with the firm for the next 41 years. When he joined, GE was considered an under-performing, inefficient, bureaucratic, and slow-to-react organization. In his 21 years as CEO, Welch saw market capitalization rise from $13 billion to $280 billion. This owes much to his strategic vision and strong leadership and communications skills.

Born: 1935, Peabody, Massachusetts
Importance: Took General Electric to unprecedented levels of growth

With a PhD in chemical engineering, Welch joined GE as a junior engineer. After just one year, he became disillusioned with its bureaucracy. Persuaded to stay on, he rose swiftly up the organization, owing primarily to his aggressive marketing style. In 1979 he became senior vice president and, two years later, he was appointed CEO—the youngest in the company's history. Faced with a large, clumsy, and bureaucratic organization that carried far too many people, Welch introduced a number of innovative reforms.

His first goal was to streamline the business. He decided to sell off any division that was not number one or number two in its particular industry—a strategy known as "fix it, sell it, or close it." It was reported that Welch sacked the least performing 10 percent of his managers, while rewarding the top 20 percent with bonuses and stock options. Of the 411,000 people employed in 1980, 299,000 remained five years later.

Welch transformed the business into an informal learning environment, encouraging his managers to see their divisions as "grocery stores," developing an ability to identify market opportunities and to react quickly and with flexibility. This strategy was complemented by the introduction of "anti-groups." These

groups were given the task of suggesting radical changes that might run counter to official division or GE policy, thereby stimulating debate. In the 1990s, Welch adopted "Six Sigma" quality management, an approach designed to achieve near perfection in the efficiency of production. Trained experts, known as "black belts," were responsible for monitoring the gradual introduction of changes that would achieve the elimination of defects.

That Welch's success owes much to his leadership and communication skills is indisputable. Holding regular meetings with his top executives and making frequent—though often unexpected—visits to his 12 divisions, Welch was always able to deliver his message in person. He also believed that the real strength of an organization lay with its personnel, and that this was a strength the competition would find hard to beat. Consequently, he spent a lot of his time meeting people and ensuring that he was involved in the annual assessment of 3,000 of his top staff.

Mavericks

Bill Gates

In 1976, together with Paul Allen, Bill Gates founded Microsoft, which in time became the world's dominant software company. This supremacy has been achieved through the development of operating systems such as MS-DOS and Windows and the Internet browser Internet Explorer. With an increase in the market value of his company in the 1990s, Gates has become the richest man in the world.

Born: 1955, Seattle, Washington
Importance: Developed and marketed the best-known operating system for personal computers

Bill Gates's fascination with programming computers began at school, where he met Microsoft's cofounder Paul Allen. At Harvard Business School, the two of them developed the first computer language program—Altair BASIC—for a prototype personal computer (PC), the Altair 8800, developed by the company MITS. The company liked, and purchased, the program. Gates and Allen, having formed a partnership called Micro-Soft, left Harvard in 1975 to pursue other projects.

In 1980, they were hired by IBM to develop an operating system for its PCs. This became known as MS-DOS and the system was licensed to other developers to make sure their programs and PCs were "IBM compatible." The success of the company was largely founded on this dependence. In the late 1980s, Microsoft released their Windows operating system, which again was a huge success and sealed Microsoft's dominance in the operating-systems market. This achievement was thanks partly to the continuing dependence of software developers on the Microsoft system and partly to earlier research and development of a similar system by Xerox and Apple.

As the dominance of Microsoft increased, so did the complaints from rivals. In 1997, Microsoft faced an investigation from the U.S. Department of Justice, having been accused of exploiting its monopoly power by preventing firms from offering applications that could run on Windows, restricting firms in developing alternative systems, and bundling software products (such as Internet browsing) with Windows. Gates argued that the pace of change in the computing industry meant that Microsoft's dominance had arisen through the natural forces of competition. The case was eventually resolved in 2002 with the government placing some restrictions on its behavior, but without really denting the power of the company.

Gates's reputation and success is based on two attributes. First, he is a technically competent executive, with a proven record in programming. (His last programming activity was as late as 1989.) He is also keen to ensure that research and development is always at the top of the list of strategic priorities. Second, he is also a businessman with a tough stance in corporate negotiations and a reputation for aggressive pricing and marketing strategies. This mix of talents has ensured that Microsoft not only weathered the information technology (IT) slump of the early 2000s, but maintained its past growth and profit records. Although no longer CEO, Gates remains chairman of the company and is now more focused on new product development. He also contributes substantially from his private fortune to philanthropic causes.

"Information technology and business are becoming inextricably interwoven. I don't think anybody can talk meaningfully about one without talking about the other."

Bill Gates

Jeff Bezos

As a Princeton graduate in computer science, Jeff Bezos moved to New York in 1986 to work for a financial company. In 1994, he saw possibilities for exploiting the commercial opportunities offered by the new Internet. He moved to Seattle, where he founded Amazon, a company specializing, initially, in retailing books. Within a few years the company had moved effortlessly into other retail markets, making Bezos a multimillionaire in the process.

Born: 1964 Albuquerque, New Mexico
Importance: Founder of Amazon, the first successful Internet e-commerce operation

Bezos became fascinated with computers during high school and decided to study the subject at Princeton University. After graduation he moved to Wall Street and began to study trends in market prices, while helping to develop a network for international trades. Soon he became interested in the possible exploitation of the Internet.

In the early 1990s, the Internet was being used mainly to exchange information between institutions. However, the number of people using the service was growing by 2,000 percent a year. To Bezos this suggested a huge market waiting to be tapped, a market that relied on the listing of a large number of lines or products. Whilst investigating mail-order catalogs, he realized that, in book retailing, there were no *comprehensive* mail-order catalogs, simply because such a document (as opposed to a "book club" type listing) would be far too large to post. The Internet— with its ability to store masses of data—was the perfect vehicle for such a task. Bezos's New York company was lukewarm in backing the idea, so he decided to set up a company of his own.

Bezos moved to Seattle for two reasons. First, he had found a local book wholesaler that was willing to complement Bezos's marketing business with the stock and distribution functions. Furthermore, Seattle had a pool of highly trained computer programmers. He set up his first site with three Sun Microstations in a garage and launched Amazon. Within three months, and with virtually no publicity other than word of mouth, he was making sales of $20,000 a week and receiving orders from the whole of the United States and an additional 45 countries. With continual improvements, such as customer reviews, e-mail verification, and customer recognition, the business grew dramatically and, in 1997, it went public. The core of Bezos's strategy was, and continues to be, a focus on the needs and aspirations of his customers: to make Amazon a "customer-centric" business.

"We see our customers as invited guests to a party, and we are the hosts. It's our job every day to make every important aspect of the customer experience a little bit better."

Jeff Bezos

Major booksellers have tried to imitate Amazon's success, but Amazon held the advantage of being first in the field. By 2000, Amazon's market value exceeded that of its two nearest rivals in the bookselling industry, Barnes & Noble and Borders. Soon, the company diversified into selling more than just books. Beginning with CDs, videos, and consumer electronics, the company went on to list clothes, toys, sports equipment, and household goods as well. The world's biggest book store was fast becoming the world's biggest retail outlet.

Larry Page and Sergei Brin

From coauthoring computer science research at Stanford, Larry Page and Sergei Brin spawned the world's most popular Internet search engine: Google. In 2006, within a decade of its founding, the company's market value was estimated at $150 billion.

Born: Larry Page—1973, Lansing, Michigan; Sergei Brin—1973, Moscow, Russia
Importance: Cofounders of the search engine Google

Larry Page grew up in Michigan, the son of two computer science teachers. Sergei Brin was born in Moscow, his family emigrating to the United States when he was six. His father was a mathematician. Page and Brin met at Stanford University where each was doing research for a PhD in computer science.

Together, they worked on a new generation of Internet search engines. Their first attempt, set up in their university rooms, was "BackRub," which searched web pages based on their popularity. The two reasoned that searches by popularity would have a higher utility to a user. Although other computer programmers were also thinking in the same way, Page and Brin were able to solve the complicated mathematics behind the analysis, and this gave them the edge.

Having changed the name to "Google," they both dropped out of school to develop the idea commercially. Raising funds from family and friends, they launched the service in 1998. It was an immediate success; within eight years it had billions of web pages and attracted some 600 million searches every day.

In 2001, the business expanded its workforce to over 1,000 employees and, in 2004, the company went public with shares priced at $84 each. Within three years the stock appreciated to $500 a share and the company's value rose to $150 billion. At the same time the company has expanded its workforce to reach 12,000 by 2007.

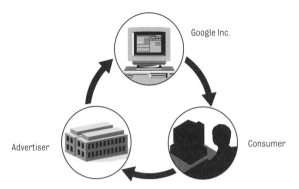

Above: The search engine business model is a little like that of a free paper. No charge is incurred by the consumer for using the service. Instead, Google and other search engines sell advertising space that is linked to individual searches. This allows advertisers to market directly to consumers already interested in their product, from whom they in turn can draw revenue.

The reason for this success is twofold. The first is that the site is hugely attractive to advertisers, given that so many searches are made each day, and revenue comes from the auctioning of advertisement "spots," which are posted alongside the search results. It is also popular with users, because it delivers a precise, efficient, and complete service. In the words of Larry Page, "always deliver more than expected." With its recent acquisition of YouTube—a popular repository for people's videos—as a further source of advertising revenue, it is little surprise that shares keep rising. However, regardless of how the company performs in the future, Page and Brin's legacy is that they have revolutionized the way people and businesses use the Internet, making it easier, faster, and more comprehensive than ever.

Monopolies

A monopoly is a market structure in which competition is very limited or even absent. In literal terms, "monopoly" describes an industry comprising a single firm—in other words, the firm and the industry are one and the same. In the absence of regulation, monopolists can exercise near total control over the prices they charge for their products and services, since there are no competitors threatening to undercut them.

Legal definitions of monopoly vary. According to British law, for example, a monopoly is defined as a dominant firm that enjoys a 25 percent share of the market. In practice, there are also a number of market factors that may constrain the power of a monopoly. They include the potential for the introduction of new, substitute, goods or services; the possible entry of powerful rivals; and the threat of government action to limit its powers.

When a monopoly is subject to an investigation, the traditional approach taken by regulatory authorities is to weigh up the arguments for and against that monopoly.

There are several arguments against a monopoly, some of which are theoretical while others are practical. Economic theory suggests that, where a monopoly exists, prices are higher and output lower than is the case for an industry where competition prevails. There is also a resultant loss of social welfare. A monopolist may restrict output in order to keep prices high, which would imply that resources are not being used efficiently and, consequently, that excess capacity exists within the industry. Furthermore, the high profits made by a monopolist are not necessarily an indication of efficient methods of production, but may just indicate that the monopolist is using its market power to raise prices above unit costs.

A monopolist can also exercise power in the market in other ways. As sole supplier it can price discriminate between different groups of customers who are separated into different geographic or product segments. This will increase revenue. It may also use unfair practices to keep potential rivals out of the market. Even if rivals are successful in entering the market, a monopolist may choose to eliminate these firms by various restrictive strategies, such as predatory pricing (designed to undercut competition) and vertical restraints (where the supply of raw materials is limited).

Some evidence suggests that technical progress is often slower when a single or group of firms dominates an industry. As it faces no competitive pressures, a monopolist feels no need to spend profits on highly risky research and development investments.

However, there are a number of arguments that can be made in favor of monopoly organizations. First, they do not always lead to increased prices, lower outputs, and welfare losses. In fact a monopoly can often lead to increases in society's welfare because of the realization of economies of scale in production and distribution. A fall in costs may be passed on to consumers in the form of lower prices. It could be argued that some industries are more efficiently organized as monopolies. Industries such as water, gas, electricity, and communications are often referred to as "natural monopolies." A natural monopoly arises when the minimum efficient size is so large that industries can only support one efficient firm. In a natural monopoly, fixed costs form a large part of total costs. Finally, far from being lazy innovators, evidence suggests that large monopoly profits are often used to finance research and development programs.

Michael Porter

Michael Porter is a management consultant and professor at Harvard Business School, best known for his pioneering work on corporate strategy. His "five forces" model is taught across the world. His interests extend to international economics and regional clusters, and he has developed an influential theory on the competitive positioning of nations.

Born: 1947, Ann Arbor, Michigan
Importance: One of the world's foremost scholars on competitive strategy

Having completed a degree in engineering, Porter earned an MBA and a PhD at Harvard Business School. His early studies were in the field of competitive strategy at the micro level, summarized in his book *Competitive Strategy* (1980). Following his appointment by President Reagan to join the Commission on Industrial Competitiveness, Porter studied the competition and economic development of nation-states.

Probably the most influential of Porter's ideas has been his "five forces model" of a firm's competitive environment. The first force is the *extent and intensity of competition*. The intensity of competition depends on the number and size distribution of an industry's incumbent firms. If there are large numbers of similarly sized firms, competition is expected to be more intense than if one or a few firms dominate. The second is the *threat of entrants*. Incumbent firms threatened by entry behave differently from those in industries that are sheltered from competition. The third is the *threat of substitute products and services*. The availability of substitute products and services naturally tends to increase the intensity of competition. Incumbents may respond by seeking to differentiate their products more strongly from those of rivals, through branding or advertising. Fourthly there is the *power of buyers*. The power of buyers of a firm's product depends on their

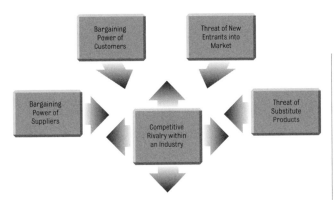

Above: Porter's "five forces" model demonstrates the factors that influence a firm's competitive environment. Competition within the industry threatens to push individual firms out, while the threat of new entrants into the market, substitute products or services, and the power of buyers and suppliers all apply pressure.

number and size distribution and their level of dependence on the firm's output. Finally, the fifth force is the *power of suppliers*. If suppliers of important inputs are large in size and small in number, they can exercise market power by raising price, reducing quality, or even threatening to withhold supplies.

Porter also introduced the concept of the value chain, which disaggregates the firm into its strategically relevant primary and support activities. The analysis examines how these links can be improved in order to increase margins on each of the firm's products. He argues that a firm must select and follow a generic strategy in order to add value and gain a competitive advantage over competitors.

Recently, Porter has focused on examining the problem of America's inner cities and has argued that more emphasis should be placed on wealth creation, rather than distribution.

Gary Hamel

Gary Hamel is a world-famous management consultant and teacher of management science. He has worked for many top companies, including General Electric, Shell, Procter & Gamble, and Microsoft. He has introduced many important strategic ideas, chiefly the concept of "core competencies." He is the CEO of his management consultancy business, Strategos, as well as Visiting Professor at the London Business School.

Born: 1954, St. Joseph, Michigan
Importance: A leading management strategist who introduced the concept of core competencies

After completing his first degree at the University of Michigan and an MBA at the University of St. Andrews, Scotland, Hamel joined the relatively new London Business School in 1983. In 1990 he earned his doctorate at Michigan. Over the course of his 25 years in academic and management consultancy, Hamel's output of fresh, challenging theories of corporate management strategy has been prodigious and widely influential.

His most famous contribution, the concept of "core competencies," was developed together with Coimbatore Prahalad. They maintain these competencies are the key to a firm's performance. Core competencies derive from a firm's specialized knowledge and the ways in which that knowledge is used in order to establish and maintain an edge over competitors. The key to staying ahead of the competition is being able to protect these core competencies from imitation. In industries where

"Any company that cannot imagine the future won't be around to enjoy it."

Gary Hamel, *Competing for the Future*

technological change occurs at a rapid pace, incumbent firms must be capable of adapting quickly and initiating change themselves. Only firms with sufficient ambition ("strategic intent") and sufficient flexibility or adaptability ("strategic stretch") are likely to succeed.

More recently, Hamel has focused on the importance of "continuous management innovation." He argues that management innovation can, at times, generate competitive advantages through the adoption of new management strategies, such as resource allocation, exploiting new markets, and motivating the workforce. These changes have the potential to ensure a firm's long-term dominance in its industry.

To reinforce his arguments, Hamel discusses the management of science, the management of intangible assets, and exploiting the knowledge of employees. For the management of science, he cites General Electric, which pioneered a new approach to managing its industrial research and design in the 1900s. Rather than rely on the chaotic and unstructured nature of research output, typical of its competitors, General Electric's approach ensured that the company gained more patents than any other American company over half a century. Hamel's example of the management of intangible assets is Procter & Gamble's approach in the 1930s to the efficient management of its various brands. Making use of employee "wisdom" is illustrated with reference to Toyota's ability to encourage its workforce teams to engage in the solution of complex production problems.

Hamel argues that, faced with the new challenges of the 21st century—the growth of international competition, the growth of consumer power, and rapid technological advances—companies should spend more time and resources on management innovations that offer newer and fresher strategies.

Ronald Coase

Over a lifetime spanning close to a century, Ronald Coase has written very little. However what he *has* written has made a major contribution to economics and management strategy. His theory on the nature of the firm developed a new branch of analysis known as "transaction cost economics," while his ideas on property rights have had an equal impact on public policy. Ronald Coase won the Nobel Prize in 1991.

Born: 1910, Willesden, England
Importance: Pioneer of "transaction cost analysis," which helped define firms and strategies

Coase attended the London School of Economics (LSE) in the 1930s and, after earning his doctorate in 1951, he emigrated to the United States, where he joined the faculty at the University at Buffalo, New York, and later the Universities of Virginia and Chicago. He retired in 1979 and is currently Professor Emeritus at Chicago. He wrote two seminal articles in his career. The first was "The Nature of the Firm," in 1937, which explained why firms exist and, among other things, gave rise to a new approach to corporate strategy. It was Oliver Williamson who reintroduced "Coasian analysis" into industrial organization, now referred to as transaction cost analysis.

The second paper was "The Problems of Social Cost" (1960), which discussed the issue of tackling externalities and the assignment of property rights. The ideas challenged the orthodoxy of government policies when dealing with "market failure" and became known as the "Coase Theorem."

In his 1937 paper, Coase observed that, in a market economy, resource allocation decisions are taken unconsciously, through the operation of the price mechanism: resources flow to wherever they command the highest price. However, for resource allocation within firms, the price mechanism is suspended: when workers move from one department to another, they do so not because there has been a price signal, but because they have been told to do so by management. Why should the task of resource allocation be assigned to the market in some cases, and to the firm in others? Coase argued that *transaction costs* are incurred when using markets to allocate resources.

Examples of transaction costs are the "search" costs associated with gathering information about relative prices, the costs of negotiating contractual obligations, and those created by governments. A firm will save on these costs if it *internalizes* the market transaction. For example, sales tax liabilities or other restrictions on economic activity imposed by government may be circumvented if transactions take place internally within the organization, rather than externally through the market. According to Coase, a firm expands when additional

> "The main reason why it is profitable to establish a firm would seem to be that there is a cost of using the price mechanism."
>
> Ronald Coase

transactions are removed from the market and are located within the boundaries of the firm. Similarly, a firm declines when it ceases to organize some transactions internally, which are returned to the sphere of the market. The limits on the growth of the firm, therefore, would be defined where the marginal cost of incorporating and *managing* additional transactions within the firm outweighed the marginal benefits.

Russell Ackoff

Russell Ackoff is currently Professor Emeritus at the Wharton School and CEO of Interact, a consultancy that deals with interactive systems design. Ackoff has published many books and academic papers and is best known for his contribution to the development of the field of operational research.

Born: 1919, Philadelphia, Pennsylvania
Importance: Major contributor to the development of operations research

Ackoff graduated with a degree in architecture in 1941 from the University of Pennsylvania. While studying there, he became interested in philosophy and was given a junior lectureship in the philosophy of science. In 1947 he received his doctorate in that field and spent the next four years teaching the subject.

In 1951, Ackoff joined a research group to develop an operations research program at Case Western Reserve University in Cleveland, Ohio. This was the first program of its kind to be offered in the United States. While at Case, Ackoff and his collaborators wrote an *Introduction to Operations Research* (1957), a textbook that essentially defined the scope of the new science. In 1964 he returned to Pennsylvania to develop the Management Science Center at the University's Wharton School.

Operations research was first developed in England during World War II, when it was necessary to organize and *manage* the war effort efficiently. The traditional approach attempted to analyze administrative problems both quantifiably and objectively in order to find solutions. However, Ackoff found that solutions to one problem often created difficulties in other areas. It also became apparent that, in a business environment, issues that confront a management strategist are often qualitative in nature, making the use of quantitative techniques redundant. Despite this,

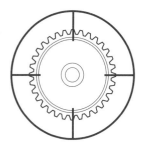 

Above: Ackoff's "synthetic" thinking concentrates on the system as a whole, maximizing efficiency by looking not just at individual components but the interactions between them. Success in one division of a business is of no use if other divisions cannot take advantage of it to improve their own performance.

managers continue to attempt to set targets according to limited quantitative measurements. Ackoff wrote, "Managers who don't know how to measure what they want, settle for wanting what they can measure" (2007).

A typical approach when dealing with a problem or issue is to break it down into its component parts. Thus a business can be examined by looking at its finance, its marketing, and its personnel functions. An understanding of each would thus suppose an understanding of the whole organization or system. Ackoff took things one step further. He realized that a system is based on the *interaction* of its parts. When examining a system, therefore, each part should be analyzed as part of the whole and not as an independent entity. Analysis will generate knowledge of *how* a part works. In order to understand the significance of that part's interaction with the whole, one requires synthesis. It is this synthetic thinking, or *systems thinking,* that Ackoff realized improves analysis of a business organization.

Robert Kaplan

Robert Kaplan is a professor at the Harvard Business School and most famous for an article he wrote with his colleague David Norton for the *Harvard Business Review* in 1992. The article introduced the "balanced scorecard," an approach for management strategists that highlights not only financial success but key non-financial performance indicators as well. This approach has since been used by many large corporations and government departments around the world.

Born: 1940, New York
Importance: Developed the "balanced scorecard" as a means of evaluating overall corporate performance

Kaplan's academic background was in electrical engineering and he later earned a PhD in operations research at Cornell University. After some 16 years at the Tepper School of Business at Carnegie Mellon University, he joined the Harvard Business School in 1984. His fundamental research was in linking the performance of an organization with its strategic goals. It was in that line of research that he developed concepts such as "activity-based costing" and the "balanced scorecard."

Activity-based costing (ABC) is a system by which business activities are broken down into their component parts in order to determine the exact resource effort each part requires. This is different from the traditional approach, which measures the overall costs of producing a product or service. ABC produces a better analysis regarding the relative costs of each activity associated with a given output.

Kaplan's balanced scorecard offered a new approach to strategic management and gave clear guidelines on the areas that should be measured to achieve an overall balance consistent with a financial perspective. The approach helped businesses gain a much clearer vision of potential courses of action. By generating information on the link between internal processes and external results, Kaplan's approach enables management to improve overall company performance.

> "Companies should decide what processes and competencies they must excel at and specify measures for each."
>
> Robert Kaplan

A company's financial measures are a record of past events and have little relevance to potential future value, which instead depends on a company's ability to evaluate its consumers, suppliers, employees, and potential for technical innovations. Kaplan suggested that a firm measure its performance from four perspectives. The *learning and growth* perspective refers to the training of employees and building an environment that is conducive to the continual acquisition of knowledge. The *business process* perspective refers to the internal business functions, which are broken down into mission-oriented functions and support functions. The mission-oriented function relies on the ability of managers to identify what the company is good at and the means by which it will measure success—for example, quality, employee skills, and productivity. The *customer* perspective measures the level of satisfaction with the company's output, while the *financial* perspective is traditionally measured by sales, market share, and return on capital. Companies frequently overemphasize the financial perspective of their business, which can lead to an "unbalanced" scorecard. Thus, for example, a company may appear financially strong yet, faced by significant customer dissatisfaction, may also be looking at a future decline in sales.

Kenichi Ohmae

Kenichi Ohmae initially joined Hitachi as a design engineer before joining the consultancy McKinsey & Co. in 1972, where he became senior partner responsible for Japanese operations. His unparalleled knowledge of worldwide industries, globalization, and international competition, and his contributions to management theory, have made him known around the world as "Mr. Strategy."

Born: 1943, Kitakyushu, Japan
Importance: A leading thinker on global competition and corporate strategy

Ohmae's first contribution to management strategy was *The Mind of the Strategist* (1983). In this book he claimed that businesses are fundamentally simple and that strategy is a question of attitude rather than rigorous analysis. He argued that a company should focus on three points: consumer, capability, and competition. Companies decide what their customers will demand next, consider their capability to respond to those demands, and judge whether they can withstand the challenge of competitors. Strategy then depends on how these issues fit together and whether a profit can be made. Ohmae argued that this contrasted sharply to American business, which is preoccupied with setting profit targets and then analyzing data to generate the necessary plans. To Ohmae this was just "spreadsheet doodling."

In the 1990s, Ohmae turned his attention to international business. He was particularly interested in the undermining of the nation-state by globalization. The ability of multinational corporations to transcend political borders was a central issue in his book *The Borderless World* (1990). In 2001, he wrote *The Invisible Continent*, arguing that technology is creating a new, virtual continent with four dimensions. First, it contains a *visible dimension*, made up of tangible products. Second, it is a

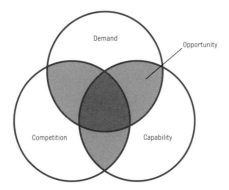

Above: Ohmae identified consumer demand, the company's capability, and the potential for competition as the three key factors in business strategy. A good strategy will aim to maximize the overlap between consumer demand and the capability of the business to meet it, while minimizing the proportion of that overlap covered by competition.

borderless world, where companies, resources, and products flow unhindered between nation-states. Third, the new technology of the Internet and mobile telephony has given rise to a *cyber dimension*. Finally there is the *dimension of high multiples*, which refers to the overvaluation that world stock markets place on new companies, which grants them the financial assets required to take over older companies. Ohmae refers to these new companies as the "Godzilla" companies, and they include Microsoft, AOL, Google, and Dell as opposed to the older "Titans"—IBM, Hewlett Packard, and Sony—who are finding it more difficult to compete on this new continent.

The focus of Ohmae's recent work has been the impact of regional economies in the new global world, which he believes is the future platform for business operations. In *The End of the Nation State* (1995) and *The Next Global Stage* (2005), he focuses on the forces that are leading to the dominance of economic regions and the demise of nations.

Multinationals

A multinational can be defined as a company that owns or controls production or services in more than one country as opposed to one that simply does business overseas. These activities can be achieved either by taking over established local organizations or by direct investment in the development of a new organization.

There are many different categories of multinational enterprise. The first is the "horizontally integrated" multinational, which produces the same product, with slight variations, in different countries—for example, Nissan and Ford. The "vertically integrated" multinational is involved in different stages of production in different countries. Oil companies are good examples. A multinational "conglomerate" is a firm that produces different products in different countries: the food company Diageo is one of these.

The important question is what attracts companies to become multinationals? There are two answers, which can be discussed under the broad headings: the potential for cost savings and the potential for growth. Companies that seek to reduce costs are usually attracted to vertical integration, while those wishing to expand their sales tend to be involved in horizontal integration or conglomeration.

The ability of multinationals to reduce costs is determined by a number of factors. First, firms may wish to seek cheaper resources, such as raw materials and labor, at source. Some resources may be unavailable in the company's home market or relatively immobile in a foreign country. Either way, the company has to locate to the country in order fully to exploit that resource. A company may also be attracted by cheap labor if it relies on labor-intensive methods of production, such as an assembly line. A notable example is Nike, which has plants in forty countries, many of them in Southeast Asia, thus benefiting from low wages. A second reason for locating in a foreign country is the productivity of labor. Although the price of labor may be higher, output is proportionately greater and thus unit costs are lower. A third reason might be to exploit advantages of infrastructure, such as good rail, roads, and convenient seaport hubs. Finally, governmental inducements—high subsidies and tax holidays, for example—may act as a spur to foreign investments. Direct foreign investment may also come about because foreign companies wish to avoid a tariff wall by locating within a customs union such as the EU.

Becoming a multinational may also appeal to firms who wish to grow. A foreign market can appear attractive if sales in the domestic market have reached saturation level. Not only will the firm be spreading its risks through such geographical diversification, but it can also benefit from various specific advantages that give it a competitive edge over its host rivals. It may have access to a superior technology, for example, or to an established brand, that will not only lead to lower costs of production, but may save promotion costs as well. Multinationals are also able to exploit superior management skills and tried-and-tested organization methods.

The growth of multinationals over the past thirty years has also been aided by a number of advances such as the development of communications, the globalization of consumer taste, and the growth of new organizational structures in managing complex global activities.

Taiichi Ohno

Taiichi Ohno joined Toyota in 1932, initially to work in the textile business. In 1939, he transferred to the automobile division and proceeded to work his way up the company. In the 1950s, he became the chief manager of the assembly line and in response to Toyota's precarious financial position, he introduced the "Toyota Production System" to generate greater efficiencies. In 1975 he became the company's vice president.

Born: 1912, Manchuria, China
Importance: The pioneer of "just-in-time" and "lean manufacturing"
Died: 1990, Toyota City, Japan

The Toyota Production System (TPS) was developed and nurtured by Ohno, who had been asked by the president of Toyota to try to match American automobile productivity. Just after World War II, one worker in the United States was producing nine times the output of one Japanese worker. Ohno claimed that his TPS was based on two influential concepts. The first was Henry Ford's book *Today and Tomorrow* (1926), which detailed his production methods, stock management, and waste reduction. The second was Ohno's observation, in the 1950s, of American supermarket operations. He noted that, as soon as shelves were emptied, they were replaced with goods—a concept that could be applied to a firm's resupply of materials in the production process.

The fundamental core of TPS was the elimination of waste and an increase in efficiency. This was important to Japanese manufacturers, since their pricing system was constrained by a relatively low demand, unlike the American pricing of automobiles which followed the "cost plus" rule. For the Japanese, where prices were fixed, profits could only rise by lowering costs through increased efficiencies.

Waste was seen by Ohno as stemming from many sources: overproduction, time spent waiting on the production line in between processes, the transporting of

> "Costs do not exist to be calculated. Costs exist to be reduced."
>
> Taiichi Ohno

semifinished goods around the plant in a chaotic, unplanned way, slow processing times, holding large levels of stock, and defects in stock and finished goods.

Ohno's solutions were labeled the "just-in-time" (JIT) system and "autonomation." JIT ensured that items moved through the plant only when they were required and at a flow that was as steady as possible (a concept known as "production leveling"). In order to control the flow of items through the plant, Ohno introduced the "kanban," a card that detailed precisely what needed to be done with a given item. The advantage of this system was that it reduced both work-in-progress and finished stock by controlling the inputs until they were needed.

Autonomation ensured that each automated process had a human dimension. If a worker spotted a problem that he couldn't fix, the production line would stop and all workers were required to help solve the problem immediately. To allow a defect to pass through might cause future disruption and waste, as production time was plowed into products that would never be sold.

The huge efficiency gains made by Toyota through TPS and JIT had a massive impact on Western manufacturing in the 1970s and 1980s. The system was adopted in many companies around the globe, where it was referred to as "lean manufacturing" or "stockless production."

Herbert Simon

Nobel Laureate Herbert Simon is best known for his contribution to organizational decision making in the field of microeconomics and corporate strategy. He argued that traditional analysis of the firm had assumed perfect information. In reality, decision makers were confronted by a business environment of uncertainty or "bounded rationality." This concept led to the development of newer theories and analyses of the firm.

Born: 1916, Milwaukee, Wisconsin
Importance: Developed theories analyzing decision-making in organizations
Died: 2001, Pittsburgh, Pennsylvania

Simon's interests were much wider than economics and management. He researched in other areas, including psychology, computer science, philosophy, and notably, artificial intelligence. This enabled him to develop theories and approaches that integrated many disciplines.

In the 1950s Simon focused on the study of industrial organizations. One aspect that stood out in the theoretical models of organizations was the assumption that all decisions were rational, ignoring the possibility of human error.

Decision makers are faced with a number of problems. When making a choice, for example, they first have to identify correctly all possible alternatives. Next they have to determine the consequences of all these alternatives. And last they have to make accurate comparative assessments of the consequences. The fact that the future is inherently uncertain makes it unlikely that correct choices could be made every time. The strategist is also restricted by the costs of acquiring information about the present. This is the concept of "bounded rationality": it is impossible for a manager to have perfect awareness of all factors when making a business decision.

Rather than focus on the maximization of profits, Simon argued that managers should instead concentrate on achieving "satisfactory" profits. This became known as "satisficing" as opposed to "maximizing" behavior. Should a manager look for the sharpest needle in the haystack, or be content with finding one that was sufficient for the job? Satisfactory profits, for example, are the minimum profits needed to keep shareholders happy. (Any profits lower than this would lead to shareholders selling their stock, leading to a fall in the market value of the firm.)

Simon also questioned the use of economic models that focused on the notion of equilibrium. This approach had been developed by neoclassical economists who saw the system operating in a quasi-mechanistic way. Simon argued that economic organizations were complex and in a perpetual state of flux, making static equilibrium analysis irrelevant to the study of an organization.

> "Human beings, viewed as behaving systems, are quite simple. The apparent complexity of our behavior over time is largely a reflection of the complexity of the environment in which we find ourselves."
>
> Herbert Simon

These views were eagerly seized by economists and management scientists, who then developed more sophisticated theories and models of firm behavior. For example, *The Behavioral Theory of the Firm* (1963), developed by Simon's colleagues Richard Cyert and James G. March, used Simon's theories to develop new paradigms for corporate decision making.

Kaoru Ishikawa

Kaoru Ishikawa's main concern was that businesses should focus on quality. In the early 1960s he pioneered the concept of the "quality circle," a group of workers who suggest improvements to the production process. He also developed the "Seven Tools of Quality," of which the cause-and-effect diagram is his lasting legacy. The advantage of these tools is their simplicity in both theory and practice.

Born: 1915, Tokyo, Japan
Importance: A major world contributor in developing business quality-control techniques
Died: 1989, Tokyo, Japan

In the early 1960s, as a professor of engineering at Tokyo University, Ishikawa conceived the quality circle: a regular meeting of employees that attempts to foster a greater level of motivation and commitment by exploiting their workplace skills, competencies, and creativities. The meetings, normally of fewer than a dozen employees, were partly training, partly education, and partly idea generation. The meetings often led to improvements in quality, suggestions for product and process innovation, and increases in productivity. According to some, the growth of Japanese industry in the 1960s and 1970s was, in part, due to the contributions of these quality circles.

Another of Ishikawa's primary activities was in the promotion of statistical analysis to aid quality. In *The Guide to Quality Control* (1986) he identifies seven tools of analysis: histograms, check sheets, Pareto diagrams, graphs, control charts, scatter diagrams, and cause-and-effect diagrams. The last—also known as the "fishbone diagram," or the "Ishikawa diagram"— is probably the most famous of his tools. It helps identify all factors that contribute to a given problem. Causes are grouped according to their level of importance. The results are drawn in the form of a tree, with the trunk representing the main problem, and the

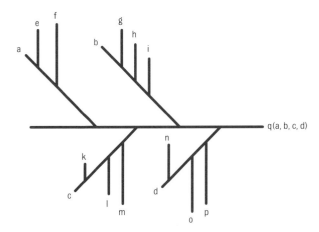

q(a, b, c, d)

identified causes drawn as branches. Typically, the main causes, or branches, in a manufacturing process are manpower, methods, materials, and machinery. In an administrative context, the main branches are policies, procedures, people, and equipment. Each branch is assessed according to its level of importance. Stemming out from the branches are twigs that represent in great detail the myriad causes contributing to a particular branch. Thus, for example, a company may wish to reduce the high costs incurred in making a product (the trunk). One significant cause (a branch) will be the high labor cost of making that product, which may be due to a high proportion of contract labor the company has to hire (a twig).

Peter Drucker

Peter Drucker is best known as a writer and lecturer on management issues who has influenced businesses around the world. It is claimed that he developed the discipline of management science in the 1940s and 1950s, resulting in a plethora of business schools and corporate management training programs. He was also a consultant for major companies, including Jack Welch's General Electric (see pages 82–83).

Born: 1909, Vienna, Austria
Importance: Thinker and author, known as the father of modern management
Died: 2005, Claremont, California

Forced to flee Germany in the 1930s, Drucker eventually arrived in New York, where he taught part-time until 1950, when he secured a post at New York University teaching management. On the basis of his book *The Future of Industrial Man* (1943), General Motors invited him to study their corporation, and this resulted in *The Concept of the Corporation* (1945), in which Drucker argues for greater decentralization and the setting of short-term objectives as a way forward. The book became a bestseller and established Drucker's reputation in the business world.

In *The Practice of Management* (1954), Drucker analyzed the corporation to an unprecedented level of detail. He claimed that, in his ten years of teaching and consulting, there was no book that covered management, and so he set about writing one, conscious of the fact that he was creating a new discipline. He saw management not in terms of an art or science, but as a profession: a profession that attempts to get the best from its resources in order to satisfy its customers.

The book posed three questions to managers: What is your business? Who are your customers? And what do your customers consider valuable? His logic was that a company's prime objective should be to serve its customers. Profit should not be seen as a main goal, but rather an important condition for survival. Furthermore a firm's relationship with employees and to society must support that primary objective.

The book is also famous for providing a blueprint for management strategy, known as "Management by Objectives" (MBO). Its rationale was to ensure that organizational goals and objectives were "cascaded" to employees and that decision making was more participative. The process involved setting explicit, measurable, and, crucially, agreed objectives between management and employees. These objectives could then be formally recorded, given a time horizon, monitored, and concluded with feedback. It was the role of a manager to assess the objectives to ensure they are coherent and consistent with the company's mission and resources, thereby achieving the cascading function. The key to these targets was that they could be measured objectively, allowing the company to develop reliable data collection and storage systems.

> "Effective leadership is not about making speeches or being liked; leadership is defined by results not attributes."
>
> Peter Drucker

Drucker's works, translated into 30 languages and spanning 60 years, have greatly influenced American, European, and Japanese business. His importance was perhaps best summed up by Jack Welch: "The world knows he was the greatest management thinker of the last century."

Alfred Chandler

As a historian, Alfred Chandler's legacy is primarily in his contribution to the development of business history as a discipline. Analyzing corporations and industries from a historical perspective allowed him to make valuable contributions to the evolving fields of management theory and corporate strategy. His main focus was on the relationship between strategy and organizational structure, and the role management played in business during the second half of the 19th century.

Born: 1918, Guyencourt, Delaware
Importance: A business historian who made a significant contribution to the theory of management
Died: 2007, Cambridge, Massachusetts

Chandler joined the faculty at the Massachusetts Institute of Technology (MIT) as a historian in 1950. He moved to John Hopkins University in 1963, and went on to become Straus Professor of Business History at Harvard Business School in 1971. While at Harvard, Chandler wrote *The Visible Hand: The Managerial Revolution in American Business* (1977), analyzing the history behind the dominance of corporate structures in the American economy.

Chandler divided American business history into two periods: pre-1850 and post-1850. For the first period, he argued that the market economy was dominant, characterized by perfectly competitive industrial structures with many buyers and sellers, no serious entry barriers, homogeneity of output, and free-and-easy access to business knowledge and trade secrets. Chandler identified three types of business for this period, which he called the "traditional enterprises." The first, the Southern plantation, had simple man-management structures and very basic accounting systems, with the owner overseeing the running of the business. The second, exemplified by Lowell textile plants, was organizationally more sophisticated than the plantation. Productivity was a key driver and managers were concerned not only with managing labor, but also with general operational issues. The third—and the most sophisticated—was exemplified by the Springfield Armory, which relied on the specialization of labor, a basic production-line system, and a divisional approach to company organization.

> "Unless structure follows strategy, inefficiency results."
>
> Alfred Chandler

After 1850, a revolution in enterprise saw "managerial capitalism" take over from traditional forms. A cadre of specialist managers took over the running of companies during this time. The railroad company, a large and complex organization, was a prime example. The complexity was solved by the introduction of clearly defined job functions, managerial lines of responsibility, and hierarchies to monitor the various tiers of management. Cost-accounting was also used as never before, allowing managers to measure accurately the profitability of the smallest of tasks and to charge prices accordingly. To Chandler, the post-1850 corporate structures led, in fact, to the *creation* of management. He also applied his ideas of American managerial capitalism to the experiences of Great Britain and Germany in his book *Scale & Scope: The Dynamics of Industrial Capitalism* (1994).

The railroad company was also the catalyst that helped the development of other industries by providing quick and efficient transportation of raw materials and finished goods around the country. The access to larger markets then allowed companies to develop production on a large scale and enjoy greater efficiencies.

Profitability

In a market economy, profit is the incentive that attracts individuals to a business. Once all employees, suppliers, and financial backers have been paid, owners manage an organization in return for the residual value. This residual should also be large enough to cover the "opportunity cost" of the owners' time.

"Opportunity cost" refers to the amount the owner could be earning if not involved in the business. The reward from an *alternative* investment or activity sets a lower limit to the profits the owner will accept. If he or she cannot earn *at least* that amount, there is no incentive to stay in the business. This is referred to as an "economic" profit as opposed to the more simple "accounting" profit.

In a free-market system, as consumers increase their demand for a product, its price rises and consequently profits rise as well. These higher, "economic," profits attract resources—entrepreneurs, labor, and capital—away from activities earning only zero economic profits (or "normal" profits). Thus profits and prices can be viewed as "signals" sent by consumers to producers and resource owners, indicating their increased wants.

Of course, firms in some industries make higher profits than those in others, which depends to a certain extent on the level of competition. Even within industries, some firms out-perform others. There are a number of suggestions as to why some firms are more profitable than others. One explanation is that profits are a reward for risk taking. In this case it is assumed that potential profits are related to risks undertaken by a firm. The higher the risk, the greater the potential profits made. A second view is that profits are related to market structure. In industries where one or a few large firms dominate, average profitability tends to be high. This may be caused by anti-competitive strategies or by firms enjoying superior production and management techniques. Finally, it may be argued that profits are the reward for a firm's past research and development investments having resulted in new revenue-generating products or new cost-minimizing processes.

An important question is whether high profits enjoyed by a firm are a consequence of anti-competitive practices or of superior production and management techniques. One view is that high profits are caused by the abuse of market power. As an industry becomes more concentrated (where a few firms account for a large proportion of total output), they find it easier to collude and erect barriers to entry in order to earn excess profits. Alternatively, firms can use individual market power to charge high prices and thus enjoy high profits. The conclusion is that government regulation is required to check the power of large firms.

An alternative approach suggests that bigger firms are more efficient (because of economies of scale) than their smaller counterparts and make higher profits as a result. Thus there is no role for government in regulating firms. Left alone, the market always corrects anomalies: collusion is potentially unstable given the organizational difficulties and the threat of cheating; likewise, monopolies, unless created and sponsored by government, tend only to be temporary phenomena. Monopolies are powerless to prevent the introduction of new goods and services. Moreover, if profits are high enough, large potential rivals will always consider entry into the market.

Sumantra Ghoshal

Sumantra Ghoshal traced the historical antecedents of the multinational and developed the concept of a "transnational company." In his later writings he presented a critique of management theory, which, he claimed, had often assumed managers were simply driven by stark economic criteria, ignoring the wider social dimension.

Born: 1948, Kolkata, India
Importance: A leading thinker in the strategic, organizational, and managerial issues facing global businesses
Died: 2004, London, England

Ghoshal began his working life at the Indian Oil Corporation. In 1981, he moved to the United States to study at the MIT and Harvard, completing two doctorates. In 1985, he joined the faculty of INSEAD in Paris and, in 1994, the London Business School. His major contribution to management was in the organization of business on a global scale, presenting his ideas in *Managing Across Borders* (1989).

Ghoshal identified three stages in the historical development of multinational corporations, each discussed within the context of a centralized or a decentralized structure. The first stage—the "European decentralized federation"—predated World War I and is exemplified by companies like Unilever, Shell, and ICI. Each foreign subsidiary within these companies enjoyed a great deal of autonomy, essentially serving a local market. The second, post-war phase—the "American coordinated federation"—included the likes of Ford, Coca-Cola, IBM, and Procter & Gamble. Though the subsidiaries operated with some autonomy in terms of production and marketing, the parent group exerted considerable influence when driving new products and technology. According to Ghoshal, the third stage—the "Japanese centralized hub"—occurred in the 1970s and 1980s and is represented by firms like Honda and Matsushita. This last group essentially focused production and technology on the domestic base in Japan, using subsidiaries as simple distribution outlets. This strategy was particularly advantageous: by concentrating production in Japan, companies were able to benefit from the efficiencies of large scale production.

"Companies that succeed are driven by internal ambition. Stock price doesn't drive them. Ambition and values drive them."

Sumantra Ghoshal

Ghoshal noted that the differences in these three stages had much to do with the nature of the industry and potential competition. Where national markets were seen as important in selling, for example, food, clothing, and furniture products, decentralization tended to be the norm. If the industry was characterized by technological change, the American model was adopted; and if the business required the benefits of scale economies with little need to appeal to national taste, the third organizational form would dominate.

The development of the "transnational" corporation in the late 1980s and 1990s saw structures that were, in effect, integrated networks of resources, skills, and capabilities. There were no organizational centers; instead, each individual unit contributed ideas and strategies that could be exploited by any other unit. By focusing on their comparative advantages and consequent specialization, units could benefit from scale economies by servicing the whole organization. The center's role was simply to manage the integration of units by creating clear objectives and developing the requisite management cultures.

Michael Hammer

With a background in engineering, it is not surprising that Michael Hammer should focus on how companies can transform their business operations. His seminal work was in the area of Business Process Engineering (BPR), which has influenced managers and altered corporate strategies around the world. *Time* magazine named him one of America's 25 most influential people in 1996.

Born: 1948, Annapolis, Maryland
Importance: World's foremost business thinker, responsible for work on reengineering business processes

BPR was developed by Michael Hammer and James Champy in their book *Reengineering the Corporation* (1993), which was primarily intended as an analysis of business operations or "workflow" through the company. Essentially, this is the study of how tasks are defined or structured, who should perform them, the order in which they are carried out, their synchronization, and how information flows are used to support these tasks.

The proposal of BPR was that, in many cases, companies were basing their workflow designs around outdated concepts of technology, resources, and corporate goals. For example, IT, according to Hammer, is misused by most managers, who look at this technology through the "lens" of the task for which they are responsible. Thus, computerization applied to an existing task, mimics a paper-based system, instead of being used as a means of generating a new way of doing things.

Reengineering forces its managers to consider radical redesigns of almost everything the company does. This revamping of the internal organization lowers costs and improves the output. Hammer argued that the chief driver for these changes should be a well-planned, well-executed IT system.

Hammer and Champy suggested a number of principles that might be considered when reinvigorating an enterprise. Most importantly, the company should organize itself around outcomes rather than tasks in different areas—production, marketing, and finance, for example. The focus should be on the complete process, from the transformation of inputs to the eventual distribution of the finished output. In this way the business could be "engineered" into various and different processes. Rather than pass work from one functional team to another, work could be redesigned so that one team would track the process from start to finish.

> "Instead of embedding outdated processes in silicon and software, we should obliterate them and start over."
>
> Michael Hammer

Other principles included a full audit of all processes and the prioritizing of those that required changes first. In addition, Hammer suggested that workflows might be integrated at an earlier stage, rather than at the end, which had been the norm. Furthermore it was important that accurate information flows were used to complement the processes.

By the late 1990s, BPR began attracting some criticism. Critics claimed the approach fundamentally assumes that the problems of a corporation stem from weak organization of its workflows and processes. Then the strategy suggests that one should "start afresh" and ignore all positive aspects of the organization—in other words, ignore the status quo. Finally it is seen by some as a cynical strategy simply to downsize the corporation in order to achieve reductions in labor costs.

Charles Handy

As a thinker, writer, consultant, and academic, Charles Handy has contributed much to theories of management and organizational behavior. One of the first professors appointed to the London Business School, he has predicted a number of fundamental changes and new trends in business and is regarded more as a visionary than an analyst.

Born: 1932, Kildare, Ireland
Importance: An important and influential management thinker; founder member of the London Business School

On leaving Oxford University, Handy joined Royal Dutch Shell. After 10 years, when faced with a posting to Liberia, he decided to leave. He spent a year working in London, in the City, and a year at MIT before joining the new London Business School in 1967, as professor of business management.

In his writings he presents his views on management in a non-dogmatic way, believing that there is no correct interpretation of the role of modern management. His first, and some would claim, most important contribution is his book *Gods of Management* (1978), in which he describes and analyzes the different organizational cultures found in businesses, each being assigned a figurative ancient Greek deity.

The first is the "power" culture, characterized by Zeus, the most powerful of all gods. In the Zeus organization, all authority and power stems from a single source, radiating outward like spokes in a wheel. This might be typical of small entrepreneurial organizations and political groupings.

The second is the "role" culture, typified by Apollo, son of Zeus, who represented order and reason. Handy sees this culture as giving rise to a well-ordered bureaucracy, where positions are precisely defined and jealously guarded. Such organizations are predictable and consistent in their decision making and change in

Above: "Zeus" organizations are controlled by a single authority figure. "Apollo" organizations rely on bureaucratic, strictly delineated areas of authority. "Athena" organizations operate through flexible interaction of a number of small teams. And the "Dionysus" model has individual teams supporting a single figurehead.

this culture may be difficult to achieve. Large companies and government departments are good examples of the Apollo type.

The third is the "task" culture, represented by Athena, the goddess of wisdom. In this organization, small teams cooperate to solve problems, with individuals and groups being granted greater autonomy to achieve results. The organization is staffed by talented individuals who are flexible and adaptable. Consultancies might be thought of as typifying task culture.

The last classification is the "person" culture, represented by Dionysus, a promoter of civilization. In Handy's analysis the organization is built around specific individuals, and its existence promotes the goals of the individuals. As a result, the organization finds it difficult to challenge and change its role. An example is a university or a law practice.

According to Handy, no culture is superior: all can produce results, and all are simply the consequence of past challenges faced by the business. What *is* important—and fundamental for business management—is knowing which culture a firm belongs to when trying to adopt new strategies or face new directions.

Tom Peters

Tom Peters began his management career working at the Pentagon and the White House and, in 1974, he joined the consultancy McKinsey & Co. He left in 1981 to become an independent consultant and to complete his book, *In Search of Excellence* (1982), coauthored with Robert Waterman. The book was a huge success and propelled Peters to the status of a modern management guru.

Born: 1942, Baltimore, Maryland
Importance: One of the world's top management thinkers

Management ideas in the early 1980s were dominated by the Japanese tradition, which didn't seem applicable to American and European business. Peters, and his colleague Waterman, analyzed 43 successful American corporations to see if they shared common characteristics for their success, and whether these could be adopted by other companies. Their general conclusions were presented in what became the bestseller *In Search of Excellence* (1982) and had a deeply significant impact on the business community. The general conclusion was that American management was failing to invest in new ideas and technology, that decision making was not shared or devolved, and that business schools were failing to develop the correct skills in their students.

The book identified eight ingredients or "themes" that characterize an excellent firm. The first is action: management must be proactive in looking for new ideas, making relevant decisions and then "getting on with it," rather than just shelving the initiative. The second is to learn lessons from the consumer. Third is the encouragement of entrepreneurship and innovation whereby "champions" are supported and nurtured. The fourth is to treat the workforce as a source of greater productivity and as a valuable asset. The fifth theme is increased management involvement in the everyday running of the company, through "hands-on" commitment. This will ensure that management will never stray too far from the reality

> "Almost all quality improvement comes via simplification of design, manufacturing . . . layout, processes, and procedures."
>
> Tom Peters

of its business. Sixth is to "stick to the knitting"—in other words, stay with what you know best, your core competencies. Peters argued that management should not be seduced by risky ventures in markets beyond its expertise. The seventh theme is to keep the organization simple and lean. Last, the "loose-tight" theme refers to the degree of freedom management should grant the workforce. Peters believed that delegation is important in the workplace to avoid managers becoming "bogged down" in the minutiae of work practices.

The book had a huge impact on management and management education in America and in Europe. Since publication, Peters has refined his views a little, to accommodate a new reality. He now believes that it is no longer sufficient to be "excellent." Instead one must stand out from the crowd, adapt, innovate, and change with new business parameters. Nevertheless, much of what was discussed in the book, and its emphasis on leadership around core values, is still relevant to today's corporation. Consequently its popularity in the business community is still very high.

James G. March

James G. March, together with colleagues Richard Cyert and
Herbert Simon, was responsible for the development of a
behavioral theory of the firm. The focus of the theory was to
understand decision making in organizations. The work was to
provide solid intellectual foundations for future
theories of management, organizational change, and
transaction cost economics.

Born: 1928, Cleveland, Ohio
Importance: A theorist who
linked psychology and
sociology in developing an
organizational theory of
decision making

March developed his ideas while a professor at the
Carnegie Institute of Technology. They were first
published as *The Behavioral Theory of the Firm*
(1963). The theory defines a firm in terms of its
organization and decision-making process. The
boundaries of the firm are loosely defined, including
all individuals or groups with an influence on the
organization's activities: managers, shareholders, employees,
customers, suppliers of inputs, as well as other parties, such as
trades unions. Management as a group might be subdivided into
groups including marketing, production, finance, and human-
resource functions, with each group emphasizing and articulating
its own priorities and objectives.

Behavioral theory is based on the observation of actual
behavior within an organization and recognizes that all decision
making takes place in an environment of uncertainty, or
"bounded rationality," as suggested by Herbert Simon in 1959
(see page 108). March argued that all decisions are influenced by
the beliefs, perceptions, and aspirations of the individuals and
groups involved, and that differences in these beliefs create the
potential for conflict. These conflicts are resolved through
bargaining processes (sometimes relying on side payments), from

which corporate goals or objectives emerge. Organizations themselves do not have goals or objectives: they are the outcome of bargaining within the organization. Corporate goals or objectives are always subject to change, as the aspirations and beliefs of various parties change over time. If a company's performance is consistently above or below its managers' aspirations, these levels may be revised, resulting in new goals or objectives. Corporate goals and objectives are, therefore, dependent on past performance.

> "The basic thesis that [March] pursued was that human action is neither optimal (or rational) nor random, but nevertheless comprehensible."
>
> Augier et al, *Industrial and Corporate Change*

Corporate goals cannot be reduced to a simple formula, such as profit maximization. In an environment of complexity, imperfect information, and uncertainty, the precise set of actions required to maximize profit is impossible to determine. Instead, the firm's managers may settle for a satisfactory profit, following rule-of-thumb decision-making conventions, which are the product of past experience.

This approach had a significant impact on businesses and business education in the 1960s, freeing management from outdated economic assumptions. The drawback, however, is that it precludes a definitive behavioral theory, as the organizational structure of every firm is different. Based on observations of actual behavior, the behavioral theory is strong on explanation, but weak on prediction, offering little more than broad generalizations as to how firms develop and grow in the long run.

Index

For main entries on business people, see contents page. References to business people are given only where they are mentioned other than their main entry.